Make Your Own Medical & Financial Powers of Attorney

A Special Request

Your brief Amazon review could really helps us!
The link below will take you to the Amazon.com review page for this legal kit. Please leave a review.

www.estate-bee.com/review8

By EstateBee Publishing

Bibliographic Data

- International Standard Book Number (ISBN): 978-1-913889-14-2
- Printed in the United States of America
- First Edition: December 2010
- Second Edition: March 2014
- Third Edition: November 2020

Published By: EstateBee Limited,
23 Lynn Road,
London SW12 9LB,
United Kingdom

Printed and Distributed By: Kindle Direct Publishing, an Amazon Company

For more information, e-mail books@estate-bee.com.

Important Note

This book is meant as a general guide to preparing your own power of attorney. While effort has been made to make this book as accurate as possible, laws and their interpretation are constantly changing. As such, you are advised to update this information with your own research and/or counsel and to consult with your personal legal, financial, and/or medical advisors before acting on any information contained in this book.

The purpose of this book is to educate and entertain. It is not meant to provide legal, financial, or medical advice or to create any attorney-client or other advisory relationship. The authors and publisher shall have neither liability (whether in negligence or otherwise) nor responsibility to any person or entity with respect to any loss or damage caused or alleged to be caused directly or indirectly by the information contained in this book or the use of that information.

About EstateBee

EstateBee, the international self-help legal publisher, was founded in 2000 by lawyers from one of the most prestigious international law firms in the World.

Our aim was simple - to provide access to quality legal information and products at an affordable price.

Our will writing software was first published in that year and, following its adaptation to cater for the legal systems of various countries worldwide, quickly drew more than 40,000 visitors per month to our website. From this humble start, EstateBee has quickly grown to become a leading international estate planning and asset protection self-help publisher with legal titles in the United States, Canada, the United Kingdom, Australia, and Ireland.

Our publications provide customers with the confidence and knowledge to help them deal with everyday estate planning issues such as the preparation of a last will and testament, a living trust, a power of attorney, administering an estate and much more.

By providing customers with much needed information and forms, we enable them to place themselves in a position where they can protect both themselves and their families using easy to read legal documents and forward planning techniques.

The Future....

We are always seeking to expand and improve the products and services we offer. However, to do this, we need to hear from interested authors and to receive feedback from our customers.

If something is not clear to you in one of our publications, please let us know and we will try to make it clearer in the next edition. If you cannot find the answer you want and have a suggestion for an addition to our range, we will happily look at that too.

Using Self-Help Books

Before using a self-help book, you need to carefully consider the advantages and disadvantages of doing so – particularly where the subject matter is of a legal or tax related nature.

In writing our self-help books, we try to provide readers with an overview of the laws in a specific area, as well as some sample documents. While this overview is often general in nature, it provides a good starting point for those wishing to carry out a more detailed review of a topic.

However, unlike an attorney advising a client, we cannot cover every conceivable eventuality that might affect our readers. Within the intended scope of this book, we can only cover the principal areas in each topic, and even where we cover these areas, we can still only do so to a moderate extent. To do otherwise would result in the writing of a textbook which would be capable of use by legal professionals. This is not what we do.

We try to present useful information and documents that can be used by an average reader with little or no legal knowledge. While our sample documents can be used in most cases, everybody's personal circumstances are different. As such, they may not be suitable for everyone. You may have personal circumstances which might impact the effectiveness of these documents or even your desire to use them. The reality is that without engaging an attorney to review your personal circumstances, this risk will always exist. It's for this very reason that you need to consider whether the cost of using a do-it-yourself legal document outweighs the risk that there may be something special about your particular circumstances which might not be taken into account by the sample documents attached to this book (or indeed any other sample documents).

It goes without saying (we hope) that if you are in any doubt as to whether the documents in this book are suitable for use in your particular circumstances, you should contact a suitably qualified attorney for advice before using them. Remember the decision to use these documents is yours. We are not advising you in any respect.

In using this book, you should also consider the fact that this book has been written with the purpose of providing a general overview of the laws in the United States. As such, it does not attempt to cover all the various procedural nuances and specific requirements that may apply from state to state – although we do point some of these out along the way. Rather, in our book, we try to provide forms which give a fair example of the type of forms which are commonly used in most states. Nevertheless, it remains possible that your state may have specific requirements which have not been considered in our forms.

Another thing that you should remember is that the law changes – thousands of new laws are brought into force every day and, by the same token, thousands are repealed or amended every day. As such, it is possible that while you are reading this book, the law might well have been changed. We hope it has not, but the chance does exist. To address this, when we become aware of them, we do send updates to our customers about material changes to the law. We also ensure that our books are reviewed and revised regularly to take account of these changes.

Anyway, assuming that all the above is acceptable to you, let us move on to exploring the topic at hand.........powers of attorney.

Table of Contents

CHAPTER 4
Creating a Power of Attorney 35

CHAPTER 5
Commencement and Cessation of Powers of Attorney 43

CHAPTER 6
The Principal and the Agent...................................49

CHAPTER 7
Alternatives to Using a Power of Attorney

CHAPTER 8
Preparing Your Own Powers of Attorney

Appendix 1

Appendix 2

CHAPTER 1

An Introduction to Powers of Attorney

What is a Power of Attorney?

A power of attorney is a legal document that enables you to appoint and authorize another person to act on your behalf and in your name. It enables you to appoint a trusted friend, family member, colleague, or advisor to take care of important matters that you are unable or unwilling to attend to yourself. This can be as simple as authorizing a friend to buy a car on your behalf, or as critical as appointing your sister to make medical decisions on your behalf if you are incapacitated and unable to do so yourself.

Did You Know

A power of attorney is a legal document by which you appoint and authorize another person (usually a trusted friend, family member, colleague, or adviser) to legally act on your behalf and in your name.

The Parties Involved

There are two main parties involved in a power of attorney relationship - the person who authorizes another to act on his or her behalf, and the person who receives that authority. The person who grants the authority under a power of attorney is commonly referred to as the "*principal*." Although they can also be referred to as the "donor" or "grantor." For ease, we use the term "principal" in this book.

The person who receives the authority to act on the principal's behalf is generally referred to as the "*agent*" or the "attorney- in-fact." To avoid confusion, we will use the term "agent" in this book.

When discussing how powers of attorney work, we will use the term "*third party*" to refer to a person with whom an agent is dealing with on behalf of the principal under a power of attorney.

So putting all of this together in an example:- you (the principal) could give your brother (the agent) a power of attorney authorizing him to buy a condominium on your behalf from a real estate developer (the third party).

Reasons to Have a Power of Attorney

A power of attorney can be used to cater for both foreseen and unforeseen events.

From a foreseen standpoint, there may be instances in your life when you need someone to carry out certain tasks on your behalf when you simply don't have the time or ability to take care of them yourself. In most cases, you will be able to find a trusted relative, friend, colleague or advisor who is willing to handle the matter for you. However, without a power of attorney, they can run into difficulty when dealing with other people or organizations who will invariably question their authority to act on your behalf. In many cases, third parties will simply refuse to deal with the person you have asked to handle the matter because of the uncertainty and risk involved.

A power of attorney avoids these problems by giving third parties the assurance they need that your agent has legal authority to act on your behalf in relation to the specific matter at hand.

Some scenarios where you might want to appoint an agent under a power of attorney include:

- You are going on vacation for an extended period and want someone trustworthy to manage an apartment building on your behalf while you are away. That person will need the legal authority to accept money on your behalf, deal with banks accounts, enter and amend lease agreements, deal with tenants, etc.

- You wish to complete the acquisition of a small business in another state and need someone located in that state to attend the closing meeting and sign the purchase documents on your behalf, as well as make any necessary filings with the relevant government offices.

- You are getting on in years and want someone you trust to manage your investments for you because you no longer have the energy or desire to do so yourself.

By using a power of attorney, you can authorise your agent to do some or all the above. Powers of attorney can also be used to authorise agents to:

- Make bank deposits and withdrawals on your behalf.

- Write checks on your behalf.

- Collect benefits owing to you.

- Claim property you are due to inherit.

- Pay your bills.

- Manage, maintain, and pay taxes on your property.

- Buy, sell, and mortgage real estate on your behalf.

- Buy or cash in insurance policies and annuities on your behalf.

- Trade stocks and bonds on your behalf.

- Operate your small business.

- Set up a trust on your behalf.

- Negotiate and sign contracts on your behalf.

- Make legal claims and conduct litigation on your behalf.

- Attend to your tax and retirement matters.

- Hire housekeepers, gardeners, nurses and so on to assist you.

Powers of attorney can be even more important when it comes to dealing with unforeseen events, especially those that leave you incapacitated and unable to manage your affairs or make your own decisions. Imagine you were involved in a serious accident which put you into a coma. What would your family do, in both the short and the long term, if they had no power to access your bank accounts, take care of your business, or even make medical decisions on your behalf? Will your financial and other affairs be stuck in limbo until you either recover or die?

In such cases, a legal instrument called a "durable" general power of attorney would allow someone you trust to manage and preserve your assets for as long as you remained incapacitated and unable to make your own decisions. Not only would such an instrument protect you, but it would also protect your loved ones. In difficult situations like this, people close to you can end up suffering and paying a high price if no one has the legal authority to manage your financial affairs and make healthcare decisions on your behalf.

For example, prior to an accident or illness, your immediate family may have had the full use and benefit of assets which were in your name alone, or even in the joint names of you and your spouse. However, after your accident or illness, your spouse may discover that if he or she wanted to sell the family car or mortgage the family home to pay some of your medical bills or the children's school fees, he or she may be unable to do so without obtaining your written approval and/or signature – something that may not be obtainable give your incapacity. The problem becomes more complex if nobody has the legal authority to manage your financial affairs as the value of your assets (and therefore your estate) may be depleted considerably if left unmanaged while you are incapacitated. A durable general power of attorney could protect you and your family in all these situations.

If you become incapacitated and have no power of attorney in place to provide for the management of your assets and affairs during your incapacity, your family may have no alternative but to ask a court to appoint someone to act as your conservator or guardian so that these matters can be addressed. This process may be difficult, expensive, time consuming and public. In addition, all these hardships will be taking place while your loved ones are dealing with the trauma of your illness or injury.

A second form of durable power of attorney, called a healthcare power of attorney, will also help things run more smoothly if you become incapacitated. A durable healthcare power of attorney gives a designated person the right to make medical decisions on your behalf when you are incapacitated. This provides clarity to the doctors and heads off family conflicts that may otherwise erupt over how decisions are to be made about your medical care. While doctors will normally follow the instructions of a spouse, if you are not married (and even if you are living with someone), then without a power of attorney there is no guarantee that the person you prefer will be the one making medical choices on your behalf.

While the odds of an illness or injury leaving you totally incapacitated may not be high, such emergencies normally come without warning. As such, a power of attorney is one of those things in life that is far better to have and not need, than to need and not have.

Types of Powers of Attorney

There are various types of power of attorney, and collectively they constitute a mix-and-match menu from which you can choose the type most suitable to your needs. They can differ based on your intended purpose for the power of attorney, the scope and duration you desire, and the time you want the power of attorney to come into effect.

You can create a financial power of attorney for the purpose of allowing a trusted person to act on your behalf in relation to financial matters such as dealing with bank accounts, transactions, etc. You can also create a healthcare power of attorney for the purpose of allowing someone to make medical decisions on your behalf if you are incapacitated.

The power of attorney can be "general," which allows your agent to do almost anything you could legally do on your own behalf, or it can be "limited" to certain specified activities. It can also be an "ordinary" power of attorney, which will expire if you become incapacitated or die, or a "durable" power of attorney, which will remain in effect during incapacity.

Finally, you can create a power of attorney that is effective immediately, or a "springing" power of attorney that will become effective upon the occurrence of a specified event.

As mentioned, you can select from these options to create the type of power of attorney you desire. For example, you could create a limited, ordinary, immediately effective power of attorney that gives your brother the ability to sell your house for you after you move overseas. Or you could create a general, durable, springing power of attorney that allows your brother to handle all your financial affairs beginning on the date you become incapacitated.

Creating a Power of Attorney

If you have reached the age of majority in your state, have sufficient mental capacity to understand what you are doing, and are not an un-discharged bankrupt, then you can make a power of attorney. A company or partnership can also make a power of attorney.

In order to create a power of attorney, you need to prepare a document stating that you as principal grant a power of attorney to your agent and specify the scope and duration of that power—i.e. whether it is general or limited (and if limited, for what specific purpose it is being given); whether it is ordinary or durable, whether it will expire on a specified date; and whether it will take effect immediately or at some specified date in the future. The document should contain signature lines for the principal and any required witnesses, as well as an acknowledgement section and signature line for the agent.

While most states have their own power of attorney forms (often separate documents for financial powers of attorney and healthcare powers of attorney), it is generally not mandatory that you use them. For example, lawyers frequently prepare powers of attorney for their clients using their own standard terminology, rather than adopting the state's official form. Banks and brokerage houses often have their own power of attorney forms as well. However, some states have specific language that must be included in a power of attorney (especially healthcare powers of attorney), so if you do not use a state's form document you need to make sure your power of attorney conforms to state law to be legally effective.

In terms of signing, witnessing and acknowledgement, different states have different requirements for powers of attorney. These requirements can vary depending on the powers to be conferred on the agent and the type of power of attorney you are executing. As a result, you will need to check the applicable laws in your state to see how your power of attorney should be executed. The powers of attorney contained in this book have been created to comply with the laws of each state.

Dangers of Using a Power of Attorney Form

A power of attorney can be an exceptionally handy tool, as you have already seen. At the same time, it's important to remember that it is a serious legal document that can have far-reaching consequences. Therefore, drawing up and signing a power of attorney is not something you should do without due care and forethought.

So while you can pick up a power of attorney form at a business supply store or at various websites online and fill it out yourself, it is not wise to use these types of "one-size-fits-all" forms without the help of a dependable book of instructions and guidance, or the advice of an attorney qualified to ask you the right questions and explain the possible outcomes. Moreover, just signing these documents alone may not be sufficient to grant authority to an agent to act for you. There are certain formalities that must be observed before your nominated agent's appointment becomes effective and you will need clear guidance on what these formalities are and how to comply with them.

So always take your time to choose the right legal book and/or professional advisors. Remember, it pays to stick with reputable brands such as EstateBee.

Scope of a Power of Attorney

A power of attorney can be almost as broad or as narrow in scope as you desire.

A "general" power of attorney allows your agent to act as your authorized representative in relation to virtually all your legal and financial affairs. This is especially important if you become incapacitated but can also be useful during periods where you are unable to tend to financial matters.

If you don't want to grant such broad authority, you can use a "limited" power of attorney under which you can limit the scope of your agent's authority by either specifically forbidding the agent from taking certain actions or by only granting the agent authority to handle specific transactions or tasks. For example, you may appoint someone to manage a specific stock portfolio but do nothing else. Or you may authorize your son to withdraw up to $5,000 from a designated bank account during the month of August to pay for his college tuition, but not more and not later.

Warning

The powers granted by a power of attorney can be broad and sweeping. It can allow your agent to do anything that you could legally do. So be sure to appoint an agent that you trust implicitly.

Duration of a Power of Attorney

A power of attorney only comes into effect after you and the appropriate witnesses have signed the document and it has been delivered to the agent (which in some states requires the agent to sign an "acknowledgement" as well). Assuming a power of attorney has been properly signed, witnessed and delivered, the agent's authority under such power of attorney will commence either on the date specified in the power of attorney document or upon the occurrence of an event specified in the document (such as a finding of incapacity, the agent's graduation from university, etc.).

If the power of attorney doesn't specify when your agent's authority will commence, then it will begin when you notify your agent of his or her appointment (provided that the power of attorney has been correctly signed and witnessed). However, as noted, in several states your agent is required to accept his or her appointment in writing before being lawfully entitled to act as agent under a power of attorney.

In most states, unless a power of attorney is stated to be "durable" it will be deemed to be "ordinary." An ordinary power of attorney is only valid for as long as you can make decisions and act on your own behalf. If you die or become mentally incapacitated, the power of attorney is deemed to have been invalidated and immediately ceases to have effect.

Durable powers of attorney, on the other hand, remain valid during your incapacity or, in the case of a "springing" power of attorney, become effective upon your incapacity. To be recognized as durable, a power of attorney should contain a clear and unambiguous statement to the effect that it is intended to be "durable." It should also contain words to the effect that "this power of attorney shall not be affected by the subsequent incapacity of the principal" or "this power of attorney shall become effective upon the incapacity of the principal," as the case may be. A durable power of attorney will remain in effect until you either regain mental capacity or die.

Provided you are not incapacitated, you can revoke or terminate a power of attorney at any time by sending a "notice of revocation" to your agent. This is a written legal notice signed by or on behalf of a person who granted a power of attorney stating that he or she is terminating the powers conferred on the agent under that power of attorney.

In addition, you can create a limited power of attorney that automatically comes to an end on a specific date or on the occurrence of a specific event, such as the purchase of a business or your return from an overseas vacation.

Duties and Responsibilities of the Agent

The relationship between principal and agent is called a "fiduciary" relationship—which is a relationship of loyalty built on trust. Your agent's fiduciary duties give rise to the following primary duties and responsibilities:

- To act in accordance with the instructions contained in the power of attorney.
- To act in your best interest and with due care.

- To act towards you with the utmost good faith.
- To avoid situations where there is a conflict of interest.
- To keep your property and money separate from their own.
- To keep accurate records of dealings/transactions undertaken on your behalf.

The obligation of an agent to act with due care does not mean that your agent must make perfect decisions or be more careful and diligent than can reasonably be expected under the circumstances. "Due care" means acting with the same diligence that a reasonably prudent person would use in managing his or her own affairs.

Keep in mind that any third party is entitled to rely on a power of attorney that appears to be valid. That means that your banker, stockbroker, and so on are protected from liability if they carry out your agent's instructions. In most cases, they are not required to check with you before entering a transaction with your agent that will legally bind you. Although, prudence ought to be exercised when dealing with agents.

It is important to understand that, as principal, your agent has the right to legally bind you and, as such, you can be legally responsible under a contract signed by your agent on your behalf. Remember, within the scope of authority conferred on your agent, he or she can do anything that you can legally do. Your agent is not required to follow your requests unless the power of attorney says that he or she must do so.

Liability of the Agent

If your agent acts in accordance with his or her fiduciary duties, then your agent will not be liable if the actions they take do not turn out the way you would have liked. As long as your agent acts in good faith, does not violate the instructions set out in your power of attorney, and acts with the care that a reasonable person would use in the management of his or her own assets, he or she will ordinarily be protected from liability. In addition, unless you state otherwise in your power of attorney document, your agent will not be supervised and will not have to report to anyone—even you.

Factors to Consider When Choosing an Agent

There is no requirement for an agent to have any professional qualifications. In general, he or she must only be an adult capable of making decisions and carrying out specific tasks on your behalf. However, your agent cannot be an un-discharged bankrupt and should not be the owner, operator or employee of a nursing home or extended care facility in which you are resident. In addition, your agent cannot be a witness to your signature on the power of attorney.

Since your agent will be acting on your behalf, will be able to bind you personally to actions he or she takes pursuant to the power of attorney, and in many cases will have complete authority to deal with your financial and legal affairs (subject to any limitations or restrictions specified in your power of attorney), the person you choose as agent should be someone you know and trust completely.

In addition, you should ensure that your proposed agent has adequate financial management and decision-making skills, as well as sufficient time and resources to handle your affairs properly. Your agent must be available when required and be able to understand your finances, objectively make decisions, execute the required transactions, and keep accurate financial records.

Conclusion

As you can see from the foregoing overview, a power of attorney is not only a useful legal instrument for accomplishing important tasks with the help of family, friends and advisors, it can be of critical importance in times of a serious illness or injury that leaves you incapacitated.

Hopefully, you now also appreciate the need to prepare both a financial power of attorney and a healthcare power of attorney to protect yourself, your assets, and your family if such an unfortunate event occurs. In the following chapters, we will provide you with enough detail to understand the issues involved and decisions required when preparing a power of attorney. You can then do so either on your own with the help of a reliable power of attorney book such as this one, or any of the others offered by EstateBee, or with the help of a professional advisor if your circumstances warrant such assistance.

CHAPTER 2

Types of Powers of Attorney

As mentioned in Chapter 1, there are several different types of power of attorney to choose from depending on the intended purpose of your power of attorney, the scope and duration you desire, and the time you want your power of attorney to come into effect. In this chapter, we will look at each type of various powers of attorney in more detail.

Financial and Healthcare Powers of Attorney

The two most common types of power of attorney are a financial power of attorney and a healthcare (or "medical") power of attorney. Together these powers of attorney allow you to provide for the management of your finances and property during periods of capacity and incapacity; as well as provide for the making of healthcare decisions on your behalf while you are incapacitated. While it may seem obvious, it is important to note that a power of attorney for financial matters, no matter how broad, does not ordinarily authorize your agent to make decisions about your health. And a healthcare power of attorney does not authorize your agent to manage your finances and other property. You need two separate documents.

In fact, some states specifically require that financial and healthcare matters be handled in separate powers of attorney. In any event, it is a good idea to do so for several reasons. First, state requirements for a properly executed and legally effective healthcare power of attorney are normally more stringent and different from those of a financial power of attorney. Second, a healthcare power of attorney will often include specific instructions regarding medical matters that are not relevant to handling your finances. And finally, people dealing with your finances don't need to know about your health matters (in most instances), and vice versa in relation to healthcare providers not needing to know about your financial matters.

Financial Power of Attorney

A financial power of attorney gives an agent the authority to manage your finances and property, and to transact business on your behalf, on the terms and within the limitations specified in the power of attorney. If the financial power of attorney is a "general" (rather than "limited") power of attorney, then your agent will normally have the authority to do whatever you had the authority to do. For example, an agent under a general financial power of attorney can:

- Pay your bills.
- Pay your taxes.
- Pay medical expenses.
- Manage your real estate assets.
- Access your financial accounts.
- Enter contracts on your behalf.
- Invest on your behalf.
- Collect your retirement benefits.
- Transfer and sell your assets.
- Buy insurance for you.
- Enter safety deposit boxes.
- Operate your small business.
- Hire someone to represent you.

If you do not wish to grant your agent authority to manage all of your financial affairs, you can create a "limited" financial power of attorney and specify what matters your agent is authorized to handle and for what period of time.

In addition, if you create a "durable" financial power of attorney, it will allow your agent to manage your finances if you become incapacitated and unable to make those decisions yourself. You can also draft your financial power of attorney so that it does not take effect immediately, but rather springs into existence if you become incapacitated.

Healthcare Power of Attorney

A healthcare power of attorney allows you to authorize an agent to make healthcare decisions on your behalf if you are incapacitated and unable to do so yourself. The authorization conferred on your agent can cover any form of healthcare decision and applies even where you are not terminally ill or permanently unconscious. It also applies in cases of temporary unconsciousness (if you were in an accident, for instance) or in cases of mental diseases like Alzheimer's which affect the decision-making process. The important point to remember is that it does not automatically terminate if you become incapacitated—in other words, it is durable (as discussed below).

With a healthcare power of attorney, you can specify guidelines and directions regarding the medical treatment that you want to receive during any period in which you are unable to make healthcare decisions on your own behalf. Save in the most extreme cases, your agent will be obliged to follow these instructions.

You can give your agent as much or as little authority as you wish to make some or all healthcare decisions for you. You can give your agent full freedom to make healthcare decisions on your behalf during any period in which you are incapacitated, or you can give specific instructions and limit their authority to certain matters.

The authority of the agent to make healthcare decisions for you generally will include the authority to:

- give informed consent.
- refuse to give informed consent.
- withdraw informed consent.
- arrange for the provision of any care, treatment, service, or procedure designed to maintain, diagnose, or treat a physical or mental condition.

There are, however, some legal limitations on the authority of your agent for healthcare. For example, he or she cannot make a decision that would be illegal if you made it, such as arranging for an assisted suicide. Even those jurisdictions that have made assisted suicide legal, such as Oregon, require that the person seeking to end his or her life make the decision personally. However, your agent can make healthcare decisions that will indirectly lead to your death, such as turning off a respirator or stopping artificial feeding.

The authority given by your healthcare power of attorney is effective only when your attending physician or physicians (depending on state law and the terms of your healthcare power of attorney) determines that you have lost the capacity to make informed healthcare decisions for yourself. If you still have this capacity, you retain the right to make all medical and other healthcare decisions.

Keep in mind that a healthcare power of attorney is different from a "living will" (discussed in Chapter 7). A living will specifies your wishes in the event that you are terminally ill or permanently unconscious and cannot tell your doctors what you want done, while a healthcare power of attorney applies when you are incapacitated but receiving treatment—in other words, when you might still get well. In most states, however, you can include in your healthcare power of attorney the same kind of instructions that you would put in a living will and require that your agent abide by them in carrying out his or her duties.

Remember also that while a healthcare power of attorney allows your agent to make medical decisions for you while you are incapacitated, it does not give your agent authority to make financial decisions for you.

General and Limited Powers of Attorney

Depending on your needs, you can create a power of attorney that is either extremely broad or very narrow in scope. If you want to give someone the ability to manage nearly all your affairs when you are unable to do so, you should use what is called a "general" power of attorney. But if you only want someone to handle a specific transaction or category of transactions, then you will want to create a "limited" power of attorney. It's important to bear in mind that you will remain personally liable for the actions of your agent under both a general power of attorney and a limited power of attorney.

General Power of Attorney

A general power of attorney is almost unlimited in scope. It permits your agent to act as your authorized representative in relation to virtually all of your legal and financial affairs, until such time as the authorization granted under the power of attorney is revoked or comes to an end. One of the most common uses of a general power of attorney is to allow for the management of a person's financial affairs should he or she become incapacitated. The need for this type of authorization may also arise, for example, if you are going abroad for some time and want to entrust the management of your financial affairs to a third party while you are away.

Important Note

A general power of attorney is virtually unlimited in scope. It allows your agent to do everything that you could legally do, in your name and on your behalf. You will be legally responsible for what your agent agrees to on your behalf. So, choose an agent wisely.

Once authority is granted under a general power of attorney, your agent will have full legal authority to make non-healthcare decisions and take actions on your behalf, as if you were taking them yourself. This could, for example, include signing letters and checks "as agent for John Smith" (a bank will need a specimen signature in the case of signing checks) or even buying and selling property, stocks, etc. As a result, a general power of attorney is virtually synonymous with a financial power of attorney.

While you cannot generally limit the scope of the power conferred under a general power of attorney, the law sets some implied limits on the agent's authority. For one thing, an agent cannot legally give away your assets (especially to himself); other than small gifts of the type that you yourself might have been expected to make, such as a birthday present to a favorite grandchild.

The authorization also doesn't cover actions which amount to matters of personal responsibility arising from the holding of a specific office. For example, an agent under a power of attorney cannot normally perform your duties as a company director (unless authorized by the company), as a trustee, or as a legal personal representative of somebody's estate. Nor can he or she take an oath or make a declaration on your behalf.

Furthermore, an agent cannot execute a last will and testament on your behalf (or amend an existing one), get married or divorced for you, or delegate his authority under your power of attorney to a third party.

Limited Power of Attorney

A limited power of attorney imposes certain constraints upon the authority granted to your agent. You can limit the scope of your agent's authority by either specifically forbidding the agent from taking some actions, or by only granting the agent authority to handle specific transactions or tasks. For example, you may appoint someone to enter construction contracts to build your dream cottage on the lake but do nothing else. Or you may authorize your agent to manage your stock portfolio but prohibit him or her from buying securities that are considered high-risk.

Ordinary and Durable Powers of Attorney

In creating a power of attorney, you need to consider when you would like it to terminate. If known, you can specify an exact date you want the power of attorney to end. If you do not specify a termination date, both a general and limited power of attorney will automatically come to an end if you become mentally incapacitated (i.e. unable to make decisions for yourself) or die. Therefore, if you wish to create a power of attorney that allows someone to manage your affairs in the event you become incapacitated, you need to make sure you meet the legal requirements for creating a "durable" power of attorney.

Did You Know

Unless stated to be durable, a power of attorney automatically comes to an end if you become mentally incapacitated or die.

Ordinary Power of Attorney

In most states, unless a power of attorney is specified to be "durable," it will be deemed to be ordinary. An ordinary power of attorney is only valid for as long as the principal can make decisions and act for himself or herself. If the principal dies or becomes mentally incapacitated, the power of attorney is deemed to have been invalidated and immediately ceases to have effect. As a result, the family of the principal may be left in a position whereby they are powerless to deal with the principal's affairs unless they seek court intervention.

Durable Power of Attorney

Durable powers of attorney continue to operate in full force and effect during the principal's incapacity or, in the case of a "springing" power of attorney (discussed below), become effective at the time the principal becomes incapacitated.

To be recognized as durable, a power of attorney should contain a clear and unambiguous statement to the effect that it is intended to be "durable." It should also state that "this power of attorney shall not be affected by the subsequent incapacity of the principal" or "this power of attorney shall become effective upon the incapacity of the principal," as the case may be—or else use similar words that show it was intended to be valid even after the principal became incapacitated.

Springing Power of Attorney

When creating a power of attorney, you can specify the time at which it becomes effective. You can either grant your agent the power to act on your behalf immediately, or state that they will only be able to act upon the occurrence of a specified future event. A power of attorney that becomes effective at a future point in time is called a "springing" power of attorney as it "springs up" when a defined event occurs. That event could include your incapacity or might be something as simple as the date upon which you complete the purchase of a piece of real estate, open a bank account, or otherwise. Springing powers of attorney can be general or limited, as well as ordinary or durable. They can even be healthcare powers of attorney.

Mutual Powers of Attorney

Mutual powers of attorney are generally made between a husband and wife, and occasionally between the partners or members of a small business or professional firm. In a mutual power of attorney, each spouse (or partner) will appoint the other (or others) as their agent to ensure that their joint plans are implemented in the unfortunate event that one of them is rendered unable to act by illness or injury.

Such documents are a legal reflection of the mutual trust and confidence which the parties enjoy within their relationship, as well as their reliance upon each other. Just as a last will and testament will endeavor to provide appropriately for one's family in the event of his or her death, a mutual power of attorney will seek to ensure the smoothest possible transition in relation to business and personal matters where the principal is still alive but unable to act personally.

Resource

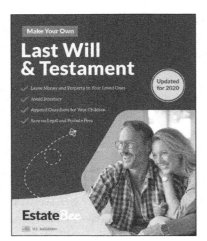

Make Your Own Last Will & Testament

By making a will, you can provide for the distribution of your assets to your loved ones, appoint guardians to care for your children, provide for the management of gifts to young adults and children, specify how your debts are to be paid following your death, make funeral arrangements and much more.

This book will guide you through the entire process of making a will. It contains all the forms that you will need to make a valid legal will, simply and easily.

Get your copy at www.estate-bee.com/product/make-your-own-last-will-and-testament/

Cascading Powers of Attorney

A cascading power of attorney is simply a form of power of attorney which allows for the appointment of alternative or substitute agents. Its purpose is to provide for a backup if the first appointed agent is unable or unwilling to act, and then further backups to replace the alternate agents if they also decline to act, or cannot act, for any reason.

CHAPTER 3

Who Needs a Power of Attorney?

The simple answer to this question is.... almost everybody. To best protect yourself and your assets in the event of incapacity, you need to execute a durable general power of attorney to allow for the management of your financial affairs; and a healthcare power of attorney to appoint someone you know and trust to make medical decisions on your behalf if you are unable to do so.

This is especially true if you have existing health problems that may make it impossible for you to handle your personal financial affairs in the future, or cause you to be unable to make medical decisions on your own behalf. And even if you have no impending health issues, an accident or sudden illness could occur without warning, making it impossible for you to take care of your finances or make critical choices.

A durable general power of attorney ensures that your agent will be able to manage the many practical and financial tasks that may arise if you become incapacitated. For example, bills will need to be paid without undue delay, bank deposits will need to be made, and someone will need to handle innumerable tasks like insurance and benefits paperwork. Many other matters may need attention as well, ranging from handling property repairs and leases to managing investments, or even running a small business. In most cases, a durable general power of attorney is the best way to take care of all these and other similar tasks.

A healthcare power of attorney gives you comfort that the person you would most want to make medical decisions on your behalf is the person who will make those decisions if you are incapacitated. It also goes a long way towards preventing confusion and disputes among family members as to who should make those decisions and provides clarity for your doctors regarding who they should take instructions from.

If you become incapacitated without having made a durable power of attorney, it is quite likely that someone will have to apply to the court to be formally appointed to manage your affairs. The persons most likely to do that are members of your immediate family.

In making an application to court, your family will be asking the court to assess your mental capacity and to decide that you are not able to make decisions on your own behalf. In those circumstances, they will also ask the court to appoint someone known as a 'conservator' (which is also commonly referred to as 'guardian of the estate', 'committee', or 'curator'). This will usually be a spouse, adult child, or sibling, and the appointee will be tasked with managing and given the power to manage your affairs while you are incapacitated.

This application to appoint a conservator is often made in public and, in some instances, a notice of the intended application is published in a local newspaper. This can be embarrassing and intrusive. If family members disagree over who is to be appointed as your conservator, the proceedings may become disagreeable and drawn out. This can greatly increase the costs of the application, especially as lawyers will need to be hired.

While the court will often appoint a close family member to act as your conservator, it is not obliged to do so. It can appoint a professional conservator who does not know you, who is not aware of your wishes, and who can legally ignore your family's requests and needs. For this reason alone, conservatorships are best avoided. Of course, you do that by making a durable power of attorney.

When a conservator is appointed, he or she will generally need to:

- post an insurance bond in case he or she decides to steal or misuse your property;
- prepare (or hire a lawyer or accountant to prepare) detailed financial reports relating to your affairs, and periodically file those reports with the court; and
- get court approval before carrying out certain transactions such as selling real estate or making investments.

The cost of doing all of this adds up and ultimately needs to be paid from your estate. Avoiding these types of costs is yet another good reason to consider making a durable power of attorney. When done right, it is a much more flexible and cheaper option compared to a conservatorship.

What if You Think You Do Not Need a Power of Attorney?

You may think that if you are married, have placed the majority of your possessions in a living trust or hold most of your property as a joint tenant, then you don't need a durable power of attorney. That can certainly be true in some respects; but in each case there is still a strong argument to have a durable power of attorney.

Marriage and Registered Civil Partnerships

If you are married or in a registered civil partnership, your spouse or partner will have a significant degree of authority to deal with property you own together. For example, he or she will be able to access joint bank accounts to pay bills, or sell stocks or shares held in a joint brokerage account. However, there may be certain jointly owned property that they cannot deal with.

In many states, a spouse or civil partner cannot sell jointly owned real estate or automobiles without the written consent of the other. Of course, if the other spouse or partner is incapacitated and cannot give their consent, the sale cannot proceed. This could have important consequences if, for example, assets needed to be sold to pay on-going medical expenses or other important expenses such as a mortgage repayment. If you were the main bread winner in your house, and your income suddenly stopped coming in, assets may need to be sold to pay bills.

If, on the other hand, you held property in your own name only rather than in the joint names of you and your spouse or registered civil partner, he or she will have no legal authority to deal with that property. Unless, of course, they had a durable power of attorney or court order.

Living Trusts

Even if you have taken the time to create a living trust, and transferred most of your assets to the trust, it is still a good idea to have a durable power of attorney.

Under typical living trusts, the person appointed as the 'successor trustee' has the power to distribute the trust assets following the death of the 'grantor'. The grantor is the person who created the trust and transferred the assets into it. He or she normally manages the trust assets until no longer able to do so due to death or incapacity. In the case of incapacity, successor trustees have the power to step in and manage the trust assets on behalf of the trust's beneficiaries.

So, you may think you are covered if most of your assets are held in a living trust. If anything happens you, your successor trustee steps in and manages everything.

Of course, one of the most common problems with living trusts is that grantors often forget to transfer all their assets into the trust, or fail to correctly transfer them in. Suppose you bought investment assets about a month before you suffered a stroke....and you simply never got around to transferring those assets into your living trust. These types of issues happen all the time. Similarly, what if you signed transfer papers to transfer assets into the trust but, unknown to you, they were invalid for some reason. Again, this happens.

For these reasons, it is sensible to have a durable power of attorney just in case things don't' go to plan.

Resource

For more information on living trusts, check out our "**Living Trust Kit**" which is available from **www.estate-bee.com**.

Joint Tenancy

Joint tenancy is a form of joint ownership where each co-owner holds an undivided interest in a piece of property. When one of the co-owners dies, the remaining co-owners automatically inherit the deceased co-owner's share of the property through a right of survivorship.

While matters are relatively straight-forward in the case of death, they can become more complicated where one of the co-owners becomes incapacitated. This is because the other co-owners will often have limited authority to deal with the joint tenancy property without the consent of the incapacitated co-owner.

Real estate provides a good example of this problem. If one co-owner becomes incapacitated, the others have no legal authority to sell or refinance the incapacitated co-owner's share of the property. In that case, they would be stuck holding the real estate on the same financing terms as were in place when the co-owner became incapacitated.

This type of problem could be avoided if the incapacitated co-owner had made a durable power of attorney. That durable power of attorney could authorize an agent to deal with the co-owner's share of joint tenancy property. That could include dealing with bank accounts, re-financings, and sales, as well as insurance and litigation matters. This would then give the remaining co-owners a means by which they could deal with the real estate. They would need the agent's consent of course, but that is something they would have to work on.

CHAPTER 4

Creating a Power of Attorney

Who Can Make a Power of Attorney?

Generally, any person who has reached the age of majority in their state, has sufficient mental capacity, and is not an un-discharged bankrupt can make a power of attorney. A company or partnership can also make a power of attorney.

The requirement that the principal has sufficient mental capacity to enter a power of attorney means that you must, if required, be able to show that at the time of signing the document you:

- were aware of the nature and extent of your assets and personal circumstances;
- understood your obligations in relation to your dependants; and
- understood the nature of the power being granted to the agent under the power of attorney.

The precise requirements for making a power of attorney differ from state to state. As such, if you are in any doubt as to whether you can make a power of attorney, you should seek the advice of a practicing attorney in your state.

Governing Laws

A power of attorney is normally governed by the law specified in the document itself, or by the law of the jurisdiction in which the actions of the agent are to be performed. Normally, this is the place in which the property or assets of the principal are located. For this reason, it makes sense to appoint an agent located in that specific jurisdiction. If you anticipate that your agent will be acting in more than one jurisdiction, you should consider making separate powers of attorney for each jurisdiction (a "jurisdiction" is essentially a place that has its own laws—for example, it can be a county, a state, or a country).

If your power of attorney is to be used in a foreign country, you may have to have it "authenticated" or "legalized" before it can lawfully be used. This is a process whereby a government official certifies that the signature of the authority (usually a notary or lawyer) on your document is authentic and, as such, should be accepted in the foreign country. For more information about document authentication and legalization, contact the local consulate/embassy of the foreign country in which you propose your power of attorney to be used.

Did You Know

In relation to states, a power of attorney made in one state is generally recognized in other states.

Creating a Power of Attorney

To create a power of attorney, you need to prepare a document containing several basic components. Firstly, it needs to contain language which states that the principal grants a power of attorney to the person named in the document as his or her agent. This will allow the agent to act on the principal's behalf and in his or her name. Secondly, you will need to specify the scope and duration of the agent's power of attorney, as well as the time the agent's authority will commence. In other words, whether it is general or limited (and if limited for what purposes it is being given), whether it is ordinary or durable, whether it will expire on a specified date, and whether it is an immediately effective or springing power of attorney. Finally, it will also need to contain signature lines for the principal and any required witnesses, as well as an acknowledgement section and signature line for the agent (which is not always required, but generally recommended).

Most states have their own power of attorney forms (often separate forms for general purpose/ financial powers of attorney and for healthcare powers of attorney), but it's generally not mandatory that you use them. For example, lawyers frequently prepare powers of attorney for their clients using their own standard terminology rather than adopting the state's official form. Banks and brokerage houses often have their own power of attorney forms as well. As long as the document is headed "power of attorney," specifies the parties, is signed and dated by the required parties and witnesses, and contains recognizable terms normally found in a power of attorney, it will be accepted by most authorities and organizations as such.

However, some financial institutions may require that your signature be both witnessed and notarized or that the document be in a form with which the institution is familiar. If you want to ensure that your agent can transact business on your behalf with these institutions, you should consider preparing two (or more) powers of attorney—one being your own form and the others being those required by the institutions with which you propose to do business through your agent, as well as those required for additional jurisdictions where your agent will act on your behalf. You should check with the relevant institutions in advance to ascertain their specific requirements and obtain copies of the forms they prefer to use. That way, you can fill in and sign their form at the same time as you prepare and execute your own power of attorney.

Signing and Witnessing

In terms of signing and witnessing, different states have different requirements for powers of attorney. These requirements can vary depending on the powers to be conferred on the agent and the type of power of attorney you are executing. For example, a financial power of attorney may have different signing and witnessing requirements than a healthcare power of attorney. As such, you will need to check the laws applicable in your state to see how your power of attorney in question should be executed.

A typical requirement for a power of attorney is to have two witnesses present at the same time as the principal signs it, each of whom needs to fill in a witness certificate at the back of the power of attorney confirming that the principal is of sound mind. One of these witnesses may also need to be within an authorized category (i.e. a lawyer or a notary), and in some states only one may be permitted to be a relative. It is also standard practice to use the same signing pen (which in some states is preferred or required to be black). Some lawyers suggest that you initial every page at the bottom to make it more difficult for the document to be altered by someone else.

For a power of attorney which is intended to be registered with an office of land titles (i.e. where the agent will be acting on your behalf for either the purchase or sale of land, or the mortgaging or discharge of a mortgage over land), the requirements are often more strict. In many cases, you will be required to have the agent accept his or her appointment in writing or have the document notarized.

Furthermore, as noted, many lending and financial institutions have their own policies regarding the execution of powers of attorney and the terminology to be used. As such, they may well refuse to accept documents that have not been notarized irrespective of whether they are legally effective or not. So, it's generally a good idea to have your document notarized as well as having it witnessed.

If you live in California, Georgia, Montana, New Hampshire, Pennsylvania, Vermont, or Wisconsin, you will need to have your agent accept his or her appointment under the power of attorney before they can lawfully act. You can do this by including an "acknowledgement of agent" section in the document and having your agent complete and sign this section. In fact, even when there is no obligation to do so, it is both recommended and good practice to always get your agent to sign this acknowledgement irrespective of what state you reside it.

In Georgia, you will also need to have your agent complete an "Agent's Acceptance of Appointment" document and attach it to your power of attorney document.

If your transactions are at all complex, and especially if they are likely to involve real estate, we would also recommend that you:

- verify the witnessing and filing requirements applicable to the particular jurisdiction/state where the real estate you are looking to buy, sell or transfer under power of attorney is located.
- make a checklist of the different powers of attorney you will need, together with an accompanying list of the signing and witnessing requirements for each one.
- at the time of signing the various documents, mark off each step as it's completed.

Did You Know

If you feel like making your own power of attorney, the sample forms together with completion instructions at the back of this book should guide you safely through the process.

Selecting Witnesses to a Power of Attorney

The witnesses to your power of attorney must be of legal age in your jurisdiction, as well as have legal capacity and be of sound mind. In addition, to make sure you satisfy state requirements, it's advisable not to use the following persons as witnesses to the execution of your power of attorney:

- your agent.
- the notary acknowledging your signature.
- a relation by blood, marriage, or adoption to you or your agent, or a spouse of any such person.
- someone financially responsible for your medical care.
- someone entitled to any portion of your estate following your death.
- a beneficiary under an insurance policy on your life.
- someone entitled to make a claim against your estate (such as creditors).
- your attending physician or an employee of such physician.

Some states also disallow witnesses who are mentioned in your will, either as beneficiary or executor. In general, you should generally avoid having witnesses who have any financial relationship with you.

Filing or Recording a Power of Attorney

Normally, powers of attorney do not require legal registration to become operative. However, where your agent will be acting in relation to any sort of land transaction, a power of attorney will usually need to be recorded or filed with the County Clerk or the Land Titles Office (the exact name of the filing authority will depend on your state). If this is the case, the document will probably need to be notarized as well.

When you register the document is largely up to you as there are generally no time requirements for registration. If it is not needed straight away, and you don't want the document placed on public record until it is required, you can hold off on registering it until the time it will be used. When that time comes, your agent can then register it. However, if you are adopting this approach, before signing the power of attorney you need to check with the clerk in the registry of deeds to see what the specific requirements are for registering. For example, in some states the documents must be a specific size or on specific types of paper.

If you intend to register your document in the Registry of Deeds in Illinois, Indiana, Kentucky, or Minnesota, you will also need to complete a "Preparation Statement." This section simply identifies the person who has prepared the document. In most cases, this will be you (the principal). However, if someone has prepared it on your behalf, they should be identified in this section.

Preventing Challenges to a Durable Power of Attorney

A durable power of attorney is a powerful legal document in so far as it grants control of your legal and financial affairs to a third party during a time when you are incapacitated and unable to express your wishes or intentions. The very act of making a durable power of attorney alone is often sufficient to create rifts and fighting between family members.

Therefore, if you suspect that your family members might challenge your power of attorney or make it exceptionally difficult for your agent to carry out his or her intended duties, we recommend that you take certain steps to alleviate some of the problems that might arise.

First and foremost, make an appointment to see your attorney. You should ask your lawyer to review any estate planning documents that you have created yourself, including your power of attorney. An experienced estate planning lawyer can answer questions about your durable power of attorney as well as questions regarding potential challenges to your last will and testament, living trust, or healthcare directive. After collecting sufficient information, your lawyer should then be able to identify whether your estate plan will hold up under the challenges of your relatives. And following the lawyer's review, you can discuss and agree on whether any changes need to be made to your documents in order to better protect you, taking into account your specific circumstances and the specific threats that you envisage.

Secondly, make sure that you sign your power of attorney in the presence of two witnesses and, even if your particular state does not require it, have you and your witnesses sign in front of a notary. Given that the witnesses themselves sign a statement to the effect that you appeared to know and understand what you were signing and that you did so voluntarily, later challenges to your competency will be extremely difficult.

Finally, you should also consider getting a doctor's statement in or around the same time as you sign your power of attorney. The doctor should be able to provide a dated statement to the effect that he or she met you on the date in question and that, in their professional opinion, you were mentally aware and of sound mind. You can attach this statement to the back of your power of attorney if you wish. Some people go so far as to have a videotape made of them executing the power of attorney and even explaining why they are doing it.

By taking the above steps, you will make it extremely difficult for anyone to challenge the terms of your power of attorney or the agent you selected.

CHAPTER 5

Commencement and Cessation of Powers of Attorney

Commencement of a Power of Attorney

A power of attorney comes into effect only after it has been signed, witnessed, and delivered in accordance with applicable state law. Thus, it differs from the general law of principal and agent (agency law), which generally allows for a standard agency relationship to be inferred from the actions and behavior of the parties. This is not the case with a power of attorney—the formalities of execution must be observed.

A power of attorney is said to have been "delivered" when a signed copy of the document is given to the intended agent, analogous to the delivery of a deed. (If you execute a deed, but then keep it in your drawer and never deliver it to the other party, it has no effect. It becomes simply a "scroll" without legal import).

A principal can also "deliver" a power of attorney by showing the signed power of attorney to various parties and institutions with whom he or she is accustomed to dealing and having the third parties agree to accept the power of attorney and to deal with the agent as well as the principal.

Assuming a power of attorney has been properly signed, witnessed and delivered, the agent's authority under such power of attorney will commence either on the date specified in the power of attorney document or upon the occurrence of an event specified in the document (such as a finding of incapacity, the purchase of a piece of real estate, etc.).

If the power of attorney is silent as to when the agent's authority will commence, then it will commence once the principal notifies the agent of his appointment (provided that the power of attorney has been correctly signed and witnessed). However, in several states, the agent is required to accept his or her appointment in writing before being lawfully entitled to act as agent under a power of attorney.

With respect to a durable power of attorney under which the agent's authority only commences at the time of the principal's incapacity, it is important to remember that the authority only commences when the principal is deemed incapacitated in accordance with the requirements set out in the power of attorney, and in accordance with state law where applicable. For example, if the power of attorney requires two attending physicians to certify that the principal is incapacitated, then the agent will not be authorized to act until this happens—even if the principal is lying comatose in a hospital ward. This illustrates why careful attention must be paid to the terms of the power of attorney in all circumstances.

Duration of a Power of Attorney

The principal may revoke or terminate a power of attorney at any time so long as he is mentally competent to do so. If it has not been revoked, an ordinary power of attorney (whether general or limited) will automatically come to an end on the incapacity, bankruptcy, or death of the principal or the agent. In addition, many limited powers of attorney are limited in duration and automatically come to an end on a specific date or on the occurrence of a specific event, such as the completion of a building construction or the acquisition of a business.

Unlike an ordinary power of attorney, a durable power of attorney does not automatically come to an end when the principal becomes incapacitated, but it does automatically terminate when the principal dies.

Revocation of a Power of Attorney

Provided you are not incapacitated, you can revoke or terminate a power of attorney at any time by sending a "notice of revocation of power of attorney" to your agent. This is a written legal notice signed by or on behalf of a person who granted a power of attorney stating that he or she is terminating the powers conferred on the agent under an earlier power of attorney.

A revocation of a power of attorney is not effective against the agent or any third party who may rely on it until such time as notice of the revocation has been received by that party. Therefore, to properly revoke your power of attorney, you should complete the following steps:

- complete a notice of revocation;

- have your notice of revocation witnessed and acknowledged before a notary public;

- provide a copy of your executed notice of revocation to your agent and request that he or she return all his/her copies of the power of attorney to you;

- provide a copy of your executed notice of revocation to any financial institutions or any other third parties who might rely on your power of attorney; and

- provide a copy of your notice of revocation to any agency where your power of attorney has been recorded (e.g. County Clerk's Office, Deeds Registry or Titles Office etc.).

As noted, if you as principal have registered the power of attorney with a County Clerk or Land Titles Registry, you should notify the appropriate authority of its revocation at the earliest opportunity in order to prevent any subsequent dealings by the agent with your property. The same applies equally to banks, brokers and other financial institutions that might have a copy of the power of attorney on their records. While some financial institutions tend not to accept or act on powers of attorney which are more than three to six months old, the issue should not be left to chance and the financial institutions should be notified of the revocation as soon as possible.

Important Note

The revocation of a power of attorney is not effective against any agent or third party who may rely on it until such time as the notice of revocation has been communicated to them.

In some states, it may be possible to revoke a power of attorney verbally. But given that a revocation of a power of attorney is not effective against the agent or any third party who may rely on it until such time as notice of the revocation has been received by that party, it is always prudent to have a written document evidencing the revocation. As noted, this document in turn can be sent (by certified mail, if deemed necessary) to all third parties who may rely on the power of attorney to put them on notice that your agent's authority has been revoked.

Reasons to Revoke a Power of Attorney

There are several reasons, both practical and personal, why you might want to revoke a power of attorney. These reasons may be that:

- the power of attorney is no longer necessary as you are now able to act on your own behalf.
- you no longer trust the agent who is acting on your behalf.
- you have found a more suitable person to act as your agent.
- it is no longer practical to have your agent acting on your behalf.
- the purpose behind originally granting the power of attorney has been fulfilled and you no longer need an agent to act on your behalf.

Remember, so long as you are mentally capable, you can revoke your power of attorney for any reason you wish. You are not under any obligation to explain the reasoning for your decision to your agent or any other person.

When Can a Power of Attorney Be Revoked?

Provided that you are of sound mind and capacity, in most cases you can revoke a power of attorney at any time, regardless of the termination date specified in the document. However, you will need to be careful if you have signed an "irrevocable" power of attorney—a power of attorney which is stated to be irrevocable during a specific period of time—which is sometimes required for certain transactions. In such a case, your revocation or attempted revocation could be viewed as a breach of contract and could lead to the agent taking legal action against you as principal to preserve the agent's authority under the power of attorney.

Determining 'Incapacity' for Purposes of a Power of Attorney

The determination as to whether a principal or agent is incapacitated is important for several reasons. With limited and general powers of attorney, the authority granted to an agent is extinguished if the principal becomes incapacitated. With certain durable powers of attorney, the agent's authority may only commence when the principal becomes incapacitated. And finally, a power of attorney will automatically end if the agent is deemed incapacitated and no alternate agents are named or willing to act. Therefore, the determination of incapacity is important for all powers of attorney.

You, as principal, will be deemed to be incapacitated if you are:

- unable to understand and process information that is relevant to making an informed decision; and
- unable to evaluate the likely consequences of making that decision.

The decision as to who determines whether you are incapacitated or not is often set out in the power of attorney document. Generally, a power of attorney will state that a doctor or attending physician (and sometimes more than one) must agree that you are incapable of making decisions for you to be deemed to be incapacitated. Alternatively, if state law allows, the power of attorney may provide that certain other specified persons (usually family members) can make that decision. By contrast, it is usually only state law which will determine whether an agent is incapacitated and unable to act on behalf of a principal under a power of attorney.

Important Note

The determination of incapacity is fundamental to all powers of attorney. If you feel you have been wrongly determined as being incapacitated, you have the right to petition the court to quash that determination.

Challenging a Determination of 'Incapacity'

If you are found to be incapacitated at a time when you believe you are not, you have the right to request a capacity review hearing by a court for the purpose of affirming or quashing that determination. You will have the right to be represented by legal counsel at the hearing.

Agents appointed under a power of attorney have a general duty to explain this "right of appeal" to you and cannot try to prevent you from contacting a lawyer or asking for a review hearing. That being said, unless the agent is a professional person accustomed to acting under powers of attorney, the likelihood is that he, she or they may not be aware of the obligation to explain your right of appeal to you. If you find yourself in such circumstances, the best course of action would be to contact an experienced attorney.

Difference between 'Incapacitated' and 'Incompetent'

A power of attorney is a private arrangement between two consenting people. As such, the determination by your doctor that you are not capable of managing your affairs is also a private one. While that determination may cause your power of attorney to "spring" into effect and allow the agent to act on your behalf, it does not affect your other legal rights. You may still be able to make decisions for yourself and act on your own behalf.

However, a decision by a court that you are "incompetent" renders you legally unable to manage your affairs. Usually, such a determination means that you cannot make contracts or decisions about your own healthcare. For example, if your conservator decides that you are going to live in a particular nursing home, that is where you are going to live and you have no say in the matter.

CHAPTER 6

The Principal and the Agent

Who are the 'Principal' and the 'Agent'?

As stated in Chapter 1, the "principal" is the person who appoints an agent to act for him or her under a power of attorney. The "agent" is the name given to the person appointed by the principal to act on his or her behalf.

The Legal Relationship between the Principal and Agent

Technically, the relationship between the principal and the agent is based on their agreement as set out in the power of attorney document. The principal gives the agent the various powers specified in that document. If the agent agrees to accept that role, then he or she must act in good faith in accordance with the principal's instructions as set out in the power of attorney document, and act in the best interests of the principal in carrying out of those instructions.

However, the proposed agent is free to decline the job and can usually quit at any time without anyone's permission. You should therefore ask any person who you wish to appoint as your agent whether he or she wants and is prepared to assume that role, as some people do not desire this level of responsibility. Therefore, some states require that the agent acknowledge in writing that he or she agrees to be the agent.

The relationship between principal and agent is called a "fiduciary" relationship—meaning a relationship of faithfulness and loyalty built on trust. One of the principal features underlying this fiduciary relationship is the requirement that the agent act with the utmost good faith on behalf of the principal. The agent can neither intentionally ignore the instructions in the power of attorney nor negligently act in the performance of them. In addition, the agent is not permitted to benefit himself or herself at the expense of the principal who entrusts the agent with the assets, as the agent is not supposed to have interests that conflict with those of the principal.

Did You Know

An agent is always required to act in the best interest of the principal and should not have interests which conflict with those of the principal.

Unfortunately, human nature being what it is, the principles of trust and good faith upon which the fiduciary relationship is built are often honored more on paper than in observance. The reality is that people sometimes succumb to the pressure of other affairs, to a lack of thought about and appreciation of their obligations, and of course to temptation. This risk of breach of fiduciary duty is the primary risk associated with agency relationships, particularly because of the agent's ability to bind the principal.

For example, numerous cases have arisen where a parent has appointed one of their children as an agent under a power of attorney and, while the parent was either comatose or on his or her deathbed, the child transferred property to him or herself. In one such case, when a property transfer of this kind was later challenged in court by the other brothers and sister of the agent, the agent argued that their father had verbally informed her that he wanted that particular piece of property to go to her rather than be split with other members of the family. The court enquired into the circumstances of each of the other family members and discovered that none of them stood to inherit anything commensurate with the property in question. On the balance of the evidence, there was enough doubt for the court to find that the daughter/agent had not maintained the appropriate standard of honesty and fair dealing. Accordingly, the transfer was struck down and reversed.

Such self-dealing is by no means uncommon. Courts tend to enforce the fiduciary duties of agents under powers of attorney because a power of attorney is one of the strongest legal authorities that can be given by one person to another and is premised almost entirely on trust and the duty to act in good faith. However, as discussed below, your agent is only required to be loyal and reasonably prudent—he or she is not responsible for every mistake of judgment.

Dealing with Third Parties

People who deal with your agent are called "third parties." For example, your agent may sign a contract on your behalf with another person, and that person is considered the third party. It is important to realize that you are the person who is responsible under a contract signed by your agent under a power of attorney that you have given. Your agent's signature binds you, and you are the one who has a contract with the third party, not your agent.

A third party is entitled to rely on a power of attorney that appears to be valid. That means that your banker, stockbroker, and so on are protected from liability if they carry out your agent's instructions. They aren't required to check with you. The only exception to this rule is where the third party has reason to know that the power of attorney isn't valid, as where he or she is aware that you have revoked it.

Most powers of attorney expressly say that people can rely on the power of attorney. Otherwise, people might not want to deal with your agent and the purpose of the power of attorney would be defeated.

Choosing and Appointing an Agent

Choosing the right person to appoint as your agent is fundamental to achieving your desired outcome under a power of attorney. This is because you are giving this person complete power to act as you would normally be able to do with respect to specified matters or transactions, for your assets and affairs in general, or even your healthcare.

Once an agent takes an action on your behalf, you probably won't be able to reverse that action just because you don't like it. The law gives your agent considerable leeway in making decisions and taking actions on your behalf and limits your ability to second-guess those decisions and actions. So, choose your agent carefully.

Factors to Consider in Choosing an Agent

When choosing an agent, always bear in mind that your agent will be acting on your behalf and will have complete authority to deal with your financial and legal affairs (subject to any limitations or restrictions specified in your power of attorney), and possibly your healthcare as well. Therefore, the first criteria when selecting an agent is to choose someone who you know and trust thoroughly.

You should also ensure that the person you choose has adequate financial management skills, decision making ability, and time to handle your affairs properly. Your agent must be available when required, be able to understand the complexities of your finances and the required transactions, be able to objectively make decisions, and be able to keep accurate financial records.

In choosing an agent, the questions you should ask yourself include:

- Does my proposed agent have the same values as me?
- Does my proposed agent have the training and experience to handle the type of matters that might arise?
- Does my proposed agent have the temperament to deal with the decisions and actions required?
- Is my proposed agent available to handle my affairs?
- Is my proposed agent trustworthy?

It is particularly important that a person who will make medical decisions for you has the same "life values" as you. Religion can play a role here. If you are a devout Catholic, for example, you may be more comfortable with a Catholic decision-maker. However, it may be sufficient if your healthcare decision-maker understands your values and preferences and can be trusted to implement them.

Values are important for business decision-makers as well. If you are a conservative investor who avoids risk, then you should choose a conservative agent. In any event, it would probably make sense to look for someone with a cautious outlook who is known to be honest to a fault, rather than a renowned risk taker. Of course, if you have specific standards that you want your agent to follow, then you should make sure that the power of attorney specifies what you want done.

If your business affairs are complicated, you may want to designate different people for different roles, such as a trusted business partner to run the business and a trusted financial advisor to manage your stocks and bonds.

Your agent also needs to be sufficiently assertive to look after your interests. A mild-mannered spouse, for example, may want to do the right thing but not have the gumption to deal with the demands of the suppliers and subcontractors of your construction business.

Distance and availability are also important considerations. However, as much you may wish that your grown children would look after you, they may not be able to do so effectively if they live 2,000 miles away.

Be realistic in determining the capabilities of your proposed agent. A brother with a drinking problem, even if he loves you, is not the person to entrust with your bank account, and a bankrupt child who stands to inherit from you may not be the best person to make your healthcare decisions.

The person you choose to be your healthcare agent should be a trusted individual who is also knowledgeable and comfortable discussing healthcare issues. Because this person may need to argue your case with doctors or family members, or even go to court, an assertive yet diplomatic individual may be the best person to represent your interests. Your representative should be aware of the choices you have made in your healthcare power of attorney and should support those instructions.

For most, the person chosen to act as a healthcare agent is a spouse, partner, or close family relative. However, despite the fact that you trust these people, you still need to consider whether they have the resolve to make the tough decisions that you have asked them to make when the time comes. If you are in any doubt, you may wish to choose an alternative agent or appoint a second agent who independently has full authority to carry out your instructions. However, we would not ordinarily recommend the appointment of joint agents as it can lead to arguments and conflicts between them which result in delays in important medical decisions being made.

In choosing a healthcare agent, you should consider the person's age, emotional ability, how well they know you, their views on your wishes and the right to life generally, their religious beliefs, whether they have any financial or other interest in your survival or death, and the availability of that person generally to act as your agent.

Finally, your healthcare agent should not be someone attending to your healthcare—there is an inherent conflict of interest in such circumstances because it is in the healthcare provider's financial interest to keep treating you rather than curing you.

What If I Don't Trust Anyone to Be My Agent?

If you truly don't know anyone whom you would sufficiently trust to appoint as your agent with broad authority over your property and finances, then don't take a chance and create a power of attorney that grants authority to someone you do not have complete faith in. In this respect, keep in mind that should you become incapacitated, a conservatorship or guardianship with the built-in safeguard of court supervision may provide the level of protection that you desire. This may be an expensive and time-consuming option, but at least it is relatively safe.

However, there is another option—hiring a professional to act as your agent. There are persons and firms with unimpeachable records that may be accustomed to providing the service you are looking for in the venue you want it to be carried out. While they'll certainly charge for their services, at least you will be able to have a high degree of faith that they will uphold their fiduciary duties, act in your best interest, and have the skills to carry out their assigned tasks.

Required Qualifications of an Agent

There is no requirement for an agent to be a lawyer or other professional person, or indeed to have any professional qualifications whatsoever. However, your agent must be an adult capable of making decisions and carrying out specific tasks on your behalf. In addition, your agent cannot be an un-discharged bankrupt and should not be the owner, operator or employee of a nursing home or extended care facility in which you are resident. In addition, your agent cannot be a witness to your signature on the power of attorney.

Appointing a Relative as an Agent

Subject to the limitations set out in the preceding section, you are permitted to appoint anyone you wish as an agent including your spouse and family members. In fact, most people tend to appoint these people as their agents because of the existing levels of trust between the parties. For example, it's quite common for one spouse to appoint the other as their agent to carry out specific tasks during any period of absence or especially during a period of incapacity.

Important Note

You are free to appoint anyone you wish as your agent provided they are a competent adult. However, make sure you appoint someone you trust and who you believe can perform the role.

However, while there are advantages to naming a family member as an agent, and there is no question that family dynamics need to be taken into account in making your decision, you have to be sure of your choice. For example, it may be appealing to name a grown child to manage your business and investments or to make medical decisions for you. However, the bottom line is that you should choose someone who can do a good job. While your spouse or child may not be happy if you appoint another person as agent, sometimes hurt feelings are just unavoidable—not to mention the fact that having a qualified agent is most likely in your entire family's best interests as well.

Agents as Beneficiaries under a Will

Contrary to popular belief, an agent can in fact be a beneficiary under the principal's will. The rule with wills is simply that persons who witness a testator's signature cannot take under the will. In many cases, people hear about this prohibition and mistakenly believe it extends to include agents under a power of attorney. But you can in fact make bequests under your will to your agent, provided that your agent does not act as a witness to the will.

Appointing 'Joint' or 'Joint and Independent' Agents

Sometimes a principal will want to appoint more than one agent to act on his or her behalf. When this is the case, the principal needs to decide whether the agents will be "joint" agents or "joint and independent" agents.

Joint agents must act together. As such, they must each agree on a course of action before any action can be taken. Furthermore, joint agents must always take the same action at the same time. If one of the agents is missing or unwilling to engage in a specific action, the remaining agents are powerless to act. This type of arrangement adds a degree of protection for the principal as it removes the possibility of any of the agents acting outside their instructions or in a "rogue" capacity.

Where two people have been appointed as joint agents, it is common for powers of attorney to state that if one dies or is otherwise unable or unwilling to act as agent, the other may then continue to act as a sole agent. Alternatively, the power of attorney may provide for the appointment of an alternate agent to take the place of the person unable or unwilling to continue as agent. Once appointed, the alternate agent will need to act jointly with the continuing agent to carry out the tasks authorized under the power of attorney.

"Joint and independent" agents, on the other hand, can act either together or individually. As such, while both or all agents may be acting on behalf of the same principal and in relation to the same matter, be it the completion of a property transaction or otherwise, they will not be obliged to consult with each other before taking an action which can bind the principal.

If you decide to select joint and independent agents, you will need to give careful thought to your selection of agents as there is obviously an increased risk that they might act inconsistently and create a mess. For many people, the better option is often simply to appoint a single trusted and competed agent and one or two alternate agents to serve if the first is unable to continue.

Alternate Agents

While it is not necessary to do so, it is always a good idea to appoint an alternate agent (also known as a "substitute agent"). The authority conferred on an alternate agent will only come into effect when the primary agent is unable or unwilling to act as agent on behalf of the principal. In such circumstances, the alternate agent will acquire full power (unless expressly restricted) under the power of attorney.

In many cases, third parties (particularly financial institutions) will require proof that the original agent is unable or unwilling to act as agent under the power of attorney before accepting instructions from the alternate agent. As such, it is often useful for an alternate agent to receive a signed confirmation from the principal revoking the authority of the original agent or, if available, from the original agent confirming in writing his refusal or inability to act as agent.

Agent Fees and Compensation

The applicable fees generally depend on who you appoint as your agent. Obviously, if you appoint your spouse or a close family member, they are unlikely to expect remuneration. However, if you appoint a professional, they may well require payment.

You can specify the remuneration that will be paid to your agent in the power of attorney itself. Alternatively, you can specify in the power of attorney that your agent will not receive any payment other than reimbursement of out-of-pocket expenses. Or you can authorize your agent to pay him or herself a reasonable amount for acting for you (although the agent has a duty to act in good faith when doing so, this still leaves open the possibility that the agent will pay himself more than you may approve of).

In the absence of specific remuneration, the fees may be prescribed by regulation. You should consult a lawyer to verify if such rates are prescribed by law and, if so, at what level they apply.

Generally speaking, it is not a good idea to allow your agent to personally benefit from managing your assets, as this creates a conflict of interest for your agent who is legally obligated to act in your best interests rather than his or her own. Of course, this comment does not apply in the case of a professional who you hire to manage your affairs and may well require a percentage fee in return. However, you should demand that such a professional be completely transparent in all their dealings and operate on a fee basis that is clear in advance.

The Powers of an Agent

In this section, we look at what agents can and cannot do pursuant to the authority granted to them under a power of attorney.

Scope of an Agent's Powers

The scope of an agent's powers will be largely determined by the nature of the power of attorney. For example, if you grant your agent authority under a general power of attorney, he or she will have the power to deal with most of your legal and financial affairs. If, on the other hand, you appoint an agent under a limited power of attorney, the scope of your agent's powers will be limited to whatever you specify, which could be as simple as a single transaction such as selling a car or piece of real estate.

It is important to remember, however, that within the scope of authority you confer on your agent, he or she can do anything that you can legally do. For this reason, it is important that you discuss the reasoning behind the grant of the power of attorney with your agent as well as what you expect of him or her. This should help ensure that there is a smooth transition of power to the agent when the time comes and that the agent is fully versed in what he or she needs to do.

Important Note

There are some restrictions on the powers that you can grant to your agent. We will take a brief look at these below. If you are in any doubt as to whether you can grant a specific power to your agent, contact a suitably qualified attorney.

Typical Powers of an Agent

You can typically give your agent authority to do some or all the following:

- use your assets to discharge the day-to-day expenses of you and your family.
- purchase, sell, lease, let, maintain, repair, pay taxes on and mortgage real estate and other property.
- claim and collect social insurance, government, civil, military, and other entitlements.
- invest money in stocks, bonds, and mutual funds.
- effect transactions with lending and financial institutions.
- buy, maintain, and sell insurance policies and annuities for you.
- file and discharge your tax liabilities.
- operate your small business.
- claim real estate or other property that you inherit or are otherwise entitled to.
- transfer property into a trust you've created (if the rules of the trust permit).
- engage someone to represent you in court or to run legal actions on your behalf.

- manage your affairs generally.

This list is not exhaustive. In fact, you can authorize your agent to do pretty much anything you can do. There are, however, some restrictions on what you can authorize your agent to do.

Restrictions on the Powers of an Agent

When you grant a general power of attorney, you give your agent the authority to do almost anything you could do yourself. However, your agent is not legally entitled to:

- perform your personal duties such as those of a company director (unless authorized by the company), a trustee or the legal personal representative of somebody's estate.
- execute a last will and testament on your behalf, without the authority of the court using what is called a "statutory will procedure".
- take any action concerning your marriage or divorce.
- appoint a substitute or successor for him or herself as an agent for you (unless expressly authorized to do so).
- decide questions of healthcare on your behalf (unless under a healthcare power of attorney).

In addition to these restrictions, there may also be other restrictions that you may wish to impose on your agent. For example, you may wish to require that your agent obtain your prior approval before effecting transactions in excess of a certain monetary value, signing certain documents, etc. The restrictions you may wish to impose will depend on your personal circumstances and are something that you need to give appropriate thought to.

Can Agents Make Medical Decisions?

Normally, an agent can only make medical decisions on your behalf under a healthcare power of attorney or under another form of advanced medical directive such as a living will. Each of these, to a different extent, allows you to choose someone to make medical decisions on your behalf if you become incapacitated or are otherwise unable to make these decisions yourself.

Duties and Responsibilities of an Agent

An agent is not obligated to act on behalf of the principal and can refuse to do so. Therefore, your nominated agent will have no duties or responsibilities until such time as he or she agrees to act. Once your agent agrees to act, however, that person will be bound by the terms of the power of attorney and by his fiduciary duties as agent.

Your agent has the following primary duties and responsibilities:

- to act in your best interest and with due care.
- to act in good faith.
- to avoid situations where there is a conflict of interest.
- to keep your property and money separate from his or her own.
- to keep accurate records of dealings/transactions undertaken on your behalf.

The obligation of an agent to act in your best interests and with due care does not mean that your agent must make perfect decisions or be unusually diligent. "Due care" means acting with the same diligence that a reasonably prudent person would use in managing his or her own affairs.

As far as keeping accurate records is concerned, the agent should keep a list or register of all:

- the principal's assets as of the date of his first transaction (or those relevant to the agent's duties, in the case of a limited power of attorney).
- assets acquired and disposed of and the date and details of each such transaction.
- receipts and disbursements and the date and details of each such transaction.
- investments bought and sold and the date and details of each such transaction.
- all the principal's liabilities as of the date of the agent's first transaction (or those relevant to the agent's duties, in the case of a limited power of attorney).
- liabilities incurred and paid and the date and details of each such transaction.
- compensation taken by the agent and the way it was calculated.

The agent should keep these records until he or she ceases acting as your agent. These records should be handed over to either the agent's successor, or if the power of attorney terminates by reason of the principal's death, to the principal's legal personal representative.

Liability of Agents

Your agent will normally not be liable for decisions that turn out badly or that you don't like, provided that the agent (i) acted in good faith; (ii) didn't violate any instructions that you specified in the power of attorney; and (iii) acted with the care that a reasonable person would use in the management of his or her own assets. In other words, your agent doesn't have to make good decisions—he or she just has to be reasonably prudent and not do anything that is clearly detrimental to you or against the terms of the power of attorney.

The legal standard for evaluating an agent's financial decisions generally favors conservative conduct. Therefore, an agent who invests your money in a highly speculative stock might be personally liable for losses you incur, while an agent who invests your money in a blue chip stock is probably not responsible for your losses, even if the stock plunges in value.

In addition, the law tends to protect agents who make healthcare decisions for others from liability, at least so long as the decision is a reasonable one under the circumstances and doesn't violate the terms of the power of attorney. That means that if your agent consents to whatever the doctors recommend, your agent will probably not be held responsible even if the outcome is bad for you.

This conservative tendency of the law can protect you from wildly speculative actions by your agent, but it can also mean that your agent may not make decisions or take actions that you would have been willing to undertake. For example, suppose that you are unconscious and there are two possible treatments for your condition—one is somewhat experimental and the other is more traditional. The agent's attorney is likely to advise that the traditional option is "safer" for your agent, even if it has a lower likelihood of providing you with a full recovery.

Finally, remember that once the power of attorney becomes effective the agent is not required to follow your requests unless the power of attorney says he or she must do so. This can create painful situations, especially if you are still capable of some participation in your own affairs. For example, you may be ill but still have "good days and bad days." On the good days, you may find it frustrating if your agent does not do what you want or even listen to you.

Similarly, you usually cannot repudiate or undo your agent's actions when you get well. He or she acts with your authority—i.e. his or her actions are your actions and are binding on you going forward.

In any event, you can only challenge your agent's actions by bringing a lawsuit, which is expensive and time-consuming. Moreover, if your agent has pilfered your money, he or she may not have enough money to pay you back. So once again: choose your agent carefully and provide them with clear instructions in the power of attorney if you have a preference as to how certain matters should be handled.

Oversight of an Agent

Unless the power of attorney provides differently, no one has a right to check up on what the agent is doing, at least without going to court. Your agent acts on your behalf, and therefore no one has any right to inquire into what he or she is doing any more than they would have the right to question your decisions about your own health or your own assets.

In addition, although your agent is your agent, he or she doesn't have to report to anyone, even to you, unless the power of attorney so requires. And if the power of attorney does require your agent to report to you, if it is durable and in effect when you are incapacitated then you obviously can't effectively question what your agent is doing in any event. Obviously, this legal situation can create an opportunity for the unscrupulous agent to profit at your expense. For example, the agent may buy an expensive car with your money, claiming that he or she needs a suitable vehicle to take you to the doctor.

Also, if your doctor says that you are not mentally able to manage your affairs, you may find it difficult, if not impossible, to hire an attorney. Although technically you still have your legal rights, many attorneys will hesitate to represent you in these circumstances. It may not be until you recover that you can fully investigate what the agent did on your behalf and take whatever action may be appropriate.

In some states, there are state agencies that deal with the exploitation of the elderly and disabled, so you or a concerned relative may be able to ask that agency to find out if you are being exploited. It is also a crime in some states to exploit the elderly or disabled.

Protecting Against Bad Decisions by an Agent

Given the limitations on agent oversight and the fact that under a power of attorney your agent will be acting on your behalf and be able to bind you personally, the most important way to protect yourself is to choose your agent extremely carefully. The second is to include appropriate clauses in your power to attorney to take care of the risks that worry you.

For example, if you are worried about the possibility of financial misconduct, you can require your agent to account every so often to another person, such as a trusted relative or friend. You can also give that relative the right to bring a lawsuit to challenge your agent's actions or to have him or her replaced.

In addition, you can specify what your preferences are for important decisions. For example, in a general power of attorney, you can forbid the agent from disposing of your family heirlooms. In a healthcare power of attorney, you may state that you want to be treated at a certain specified hospital unless your condition demands otherwise.

There may also be times when it makes sense to appoint two or more persons to serve as joint agents. This may make it more difficult to get decisions made if they disagree, but it may give you needed protection from one of them acting wrongfully.

Finally, you can require your agent for financial matters to post a bond if you think it is appropriate under the circumstances.

CHAPTER 7

Alternatives to Using a Power of Attorney

Although in many situations a power or attorney is the best way to appoint another person to act on your behalf, in some circumstances there are alternatives which may be preferable to a power of attorney, or can act in tandem with a power of attorney. In this chapter we will review a couple of these options so that you are aware of your choices.

Standard Agency Relationships

As we have described in detail throughout this book, a power of attorney creates the strongest form of agency relationship between you as principal and your agent. However, there are situations in which a power of attorney would be overkill and a standard agency relationship is all that is necessary. For example, the post office or pharmacy will probably allow your agent to pick up a parcel or a prescription on your behalf if he or she shows some ID and signs for the item. Or if you own a business, your sales agents can enter into agreements with your customers if they are within the reasonable scope of the agents' authority.

A standard agency relationship may be created by written or spoken words, or even by conduct which points to a relationship of principal and agent between the parties. There are times when simply asking someone to perform a task for you is all that's needed to get it done. Or you can have a more formal written agreement spelling out the agent's responsibilities and limits of authority. In either event, if the person agrees to accept the task as described, they will for that purpose become your "agent" and various rights and obligations will be deemed to arise between the two of you. A third party who then deals with your agent is in effect dealing with you.

As we just mentioned, one of the most common forms of a standard agency relationship is between a business owner and a sales agent. Another would be a real estate firm acting as an agent for a landlord, who assigns the firm the responsibility for advertising the property for rent, showing the property, checking a tenant's bona fides, accepting rental payments, arranging small repairs and the like, then deducting their own commission and accounting to the landlord for the balance.

Within various artistic, creative and sporting fields of endeavor, there is a class of persons who represent the "talent" in negotiating contracts for their clients, accepting payments for their clients' services, and accounting to their clients for the balance after agency commissions and expenses. These people are literary agents, theatrical agents, sporting agents, managers and so on.

In each case, a standard agency arrangement is a fiduciary relationship the same as under a power of attorney. This means that the principal and the agent must act in complete good faith towards each other and apply strict standards of loyalty, honesty and candor in all dealings with the other party. Thus, an agent has a duty not to unjustly enrich him or herself from the relationship, and the principal has a duty to indemnify an agent against any loss suffered by the agent while acting within the terms of his or her authority.

Whether or not a standard agency arrangement is sufficient under any given circumstances will be driven largely by whether third parties will accept such a relationship and deal with your agent. One of the main advantages of acting under a power of attorney, as opposed to a standard agency agreement, is that people generally recognize the weight of law behind it and agree to let your agent act on your behalf.

By way of illustration, consider the example of an agent who is asked to deal with some banking business on behalf of his principal. The agent goes to the principal's bank with no formal documentation and asks to be registered as a signatory on the principal's bank account. He clearly and diligently explains to the bank officer that his principal asked him to do his banking and pay his bills while he's unable to do so, and then reaches for his signing pen to withdraw some money. The chances of the bank acceding to the agent's request are slim to none, as you'd no doubt agree.

However, if the agent approaches the bank officer with a formal, properly executed and notarized power of attorney, there is a good chance the bank will allow the agent to proceed as requested (unless the bank requires its own form of power of attorney—which you should anticipate when granting a financial power of attorney to your agent and use the appropriate form).

If you picture similar scenarios playing out between your agent and your stockbroker, real estate agent, insurer, etc., you can once again see the value of creating a power of attorney.

Living Trusts

A trust is a legally recognized fiduciary arrangement whereby a person (the "grantor" or the "settlor") places property in trust for the benefit of another person or persons (the "beneficiary" or "beneficiaries"). The property is legally owned, controlled and managed by a "trustee," who can be either the grantor or a third person and who has a fiduciary obligation to hold and administer the trust assets for the benefit of the beneficiary or beneficiaries. The terms of a trust, including how the property is to be managed and when and how it will be distributed to the beneficiaries, are usually set out in a trust document.

You can create what is called a "living trust" (also known as an "inter vivos" trust) whereby you as grantor are the initial trustee and in complete control over the property until a specified event occurs, upon which time your designated "successor trustee" takes over management of the assets. Your successor trustee is the person who assumes control of the trust after you, as initial trustee, become incapacitated and/or die. A successor trustee has no authority to act while any of the grantors remain alive or capable of managing the trust. Your trust agreement will identify the person or persons who will act as successor trustee(s) of your trust.

While it is not within the scope of this book to provide a comprehensive list of a successor trustee's duties, it is useful for you to have an understanding of their role and duties so that you can decide who is best for the role. As with an agent under a power of attorney, the successor trustee of your living trust owes the beneficiaries of the trust a fiduciary duty.

Some specific aspects of the fiduciary duty of a successor trustee include the duty to:

- adhere to the terms of the trust.
- act personally in the management and administration of the trust.
- act in the best interests of the beneficiaries of the trust.
- supply information regarding the trust and its assets to the beneficiaries.
- invest prudently.
- keep trust assets separate from those of the successor trustee.
- carry out the role of trustee without payment—unless the terms of the trust provide otherwise, or the trustee is a professional trustee.

As creator of the living trust you can, at any time, either revoke the trust or call for the return of some or all the property transferred to it. You can also add assets to the trust, change the terms of the trust, change the successor trustee and beneficiaries, and even make it irrevocable (incapable of change) at any time in the future. After your death, your successor trustee will distribute the proceeds of the trust to the named beneficiaries in accordance with the terms of the trust agreement.

A living trust can be set up to act very much like a durable power of attorney, where a grantor appoints a family member, friend or advisor to manage his or her financial assets in the event he or she becomes incapacitated. Also like a power of attorney, the powers of a trustee who is not the grantor can be established as broad or as limited as the grantor sees fit, can exist at the creation of the trust or can "spring" into existence upon the happening of a certain event, can terminate upon a certain date or the occurrence of a certain event, and be revoked by the grantor at any time (assuming it is not an irrevocable trust).

A trust, however, has several advantages over a power of attorney. One advantage is that placing assets in a properly constructed trust allows them to pass outside of the time-consuming and expensive process of probate (the legal process by which a person's estate is administered and distributed under a will, and which is usually carried out under court supervision) after his or her death. Another is that a properly constructed trust may result in significant beneficial tax consequences for the grantor and the beneficiaries.

But for the purposes of your ability to have a friend, family member or advisor manage your financial affairs when you are unable to do so for yourself, the main advantage of a trust is the ability to have your designated person continue taking care of your assets beyond the time of your death. As we have discussed, a power of attorney always expires when the principal dies, and therefore the agent at that time can no longer manage the principal's assets. A trust, on the other hand, can survive the death of the grantor, and therefore the successor trustee is able to continue to manage the assets for the benefit of the beneficiaries until they are distributed.

For example, let's assume your primary assets consist of several pieces of real estate and a portfolio of securities, and that you currently have a will under which you leave all your property to certain beneficiaries. If you give your brother a durable general power of attorney that will spring into effect when you become incapacitated, then he will be able to manage your real estate, securities and other assets if an accident or illness does not allow you to do so for yourself. But if you die, the power of attorney is automatically terminated, and these valuable assets will all be in limbo while they go through probate and pass to your beneficiaries under your will.

However, using the same example, if you create a living trust with you as initial trustee, and your brother as successor trustee in the event you become incapacitated or pass away, and you put your real estate, securities, and other valuable assets into the trust, then if you become incapacitated your brother can manage these assets on behalf of the beneficiaries just like with a power of attorney. What's more, he can continue to do so if you die. This will allow him to maintain continuous oversight over your most valuable assets, allow these assets to pass outside of probate and more quickly to the beneficiaries, and possibly result in significant tax savings if the trust is properly structured.

You may also decide, either at the creation of your trust or at a later date, that you would prefer to nominate a person other than yourself to act as trustee of the trust at a time when you still have the ability to do so yourself. That is perfectly fine as the trustee will be obliged to act in accordance with your instructions as grantor of the trust—provided the instructions are legal—as well as his or her fiduciary duties.

However, if someone else is acting as trustee of your trust, they will need to obtain an identification number from the Internal Revenue Service (IRS) for the trust and thereafter make income tax returns on behalf of the trust. In addition, we recommend that you see a lawyer if you choose not to act as trustee of your own trust at the outset. The removal of day-to-day control over your assets could have significant legal, financial, and practical consequences.

You may also decide, for whatever reason, that rather than hand over the management of your trust assets to another person entirely, you would simply like to engage someone to assist in the management of your trust property. You can do this by appointing another person as a co-trustee of your trust. As co-trustees, both of you would have authority to act on the trust's behalf. Again, while there is no real difficulty with having someone else act as trustee of your trust or having someone act as a co-trustee, we recommend that you speak to a lawyer before you do this, as the terms of your trust document may need to be tailored to having someone other than yourself as a trustee.

One of the biggest problems associated with living trusts is the failure to properly transfer assets into the trust itself. This act of transferring assets is commonly referred to as "funding the trust." Where the assets are not properly transferred to the trust, they are not subject to the terms of your trust. That means they cannot be legally managed by your successor trustee, and they also remain part of your probate estate. In addition, if you have not provided for the transfer of these assets under your will, which is likely, they may end up being unintentionally gifted to the person entitled to the residue of your estate under your will or, where there is no will, to a relative by intestacy.

Therefore, if any of the assets you propose transferring to your trust have forms of "title documents" associated with them, you must ensure that the title is properly transferred from your personal name into the name of the trustee, acting as such on behalf of the trust.

Remember, a trust is not a legal entity—it is simply the legal relationship between the grantor and the trustee. Therefore, a trust cannot hold title to property such as real estate, bank accounts, etc. in its own name (the way a corporation can, for example). It is the trustee rather that must hold legal title to the trust assets, with the beneficiaries holding what is called "equitable" or beneficial title. Since the trustee holds legal title to the trust assets, those assets are always held in the trustee's name—albeit "as trustee" for the designated trust. So when we refer to assets being transferred to a trust, this means that legal title to those assets is being transferred to the trustee to be held in trust in accordance with the agreement between the grantor and the trustee.

To transfer assets which do not have title documents to your trust, all you typically need to do is simply list them in the schedule of assets contained at the back of your trust agreement.

Resource

For further information on assets that do not go through probate, see: **Make Your Own Living Trust & Avoid Probate**

Living trusts are used to distribute a person's assets after they die in a manner that avoids the costs, delays, and publicity of probate. They also cater for the management of property during periods of incapacity.

This book will guide you step-by-step through the process of creating your very own living trust, transferring assets to your living trust, and subsequently managing those assets. All relevant forms are included.

Get your copy at www.estate-bee.com/product/make-your-own-living-trust-avoid-probate/

With respect to assets which do have title documents, we recommend that all these assets be re-titled in the following manner. To change the title of an asset from your personal name to the name of the trustee for your living trust, you simply sign a document transferring the legal title in that asset from you to the trustee. The transfer will be between, for example, John Smith and John Smith, trustee of the John Smith Family living trust dated January 1, 2021. Then when it comes to signing the transfer document, you will sign the document in your own right as (for example) "John Smith," and you will also sign on behalf of the living trust using the words "John Smith, Trustee."

Be aware, however, that trusts having all the benefits described in this section are sometimes complex and not easy to establish. And if a trust is not created properly there could be substantial adverse effects. For more detailed information, see "Make Your Own Living Trust & Avoid Probate" by EstateBee. In addition, it is also recommended that you consult an experienced attorney and/or tax advisor when establishing a trust into which you will place valuable assets.

Living Wills

Both a living will and a healthcare power or attorney are forms of what is called an advance medical directive ("AMD"). An AMD is a written statement in which you set out the medical care that you wish to receive during any period in which you are unable to make decisions on your own behalf. You can use AMDs to set out your preferences in relation to the receipt and non-receipt of various types of medical treatments and procedures, including life sustaining procedures. These preferences will ordinarily be honored by medical personnel if you are admitted to a hospital or healthcare facility; assuming of course they have a copy of your AMD.

In the absence of having an AMD, state laws will generally allow your close family members to make medical decisions for you during any period in which you are incapacitated and unable to make decisions on your own behalf. While this can of course be beneficial for you, there is always a risk that your family members will make decisions based on what they believe is best for you rather than what you would have actually wanted in the circumstances. More importantly, there is the added risk that the person making these decisions for you might not be the person that you would have entrusted this responsibility to had you the choice.

It was in anticipation of these very issues that AMDs were developed. Thankfully, all states now have provisions that allow for the use of AMDs so that people can exercise some control over the medical treatment they receive during periods of incapacity. The most common types of AMD currently in use include a living will and a durable power of attorney for healthcare. We've already discussed a healthcare power of attorney in detail and will now discuss a living will.

A living will is a legal document that allows you to express your preferences regarding the receipt or non-receipt of certain life-prolonging medical procedures in the event that you become terminally ill or permanently unconscious and unable to communicate your own wishes. Apart from allowing you to specify your preferences in this respect, it also allows you to designate an agent who has authority to either enforce or revoke the terms of your AMD should the agent feel that the circumstances warrant.

In understanding how living wills work in practice, it's important that you realize that living wills only come into effect when:

- you are suffering from a terminal condition or a persistent comatose condition or are in a permanent vegetative state;
- there is no real prospect of your recovery; and
- you are unable to make and communicate your own healthcare decisions.

Only at this point will the person nominated under your living will have any ability to enforce or revoke any of the instructions that you have set out in your living will. However, the law in the majority of states (and indeed the terms of most living wills) requires that before your nominated person can lawfully act, one or two physicians must first personally examine you and agree that you satisfy the conditions referred to above and that the application of medical procedures would only prolong the dying process. If the doctor or both doctors determine and agree that this is the case, then the medical procedures may be withdrawn or applied, depending on the choices expressed in your living will.

Whether or not you decide to make a living will is completely up to you. In making that decision, you will need to consider situations that might leave you in a persistent state of unconsciousness or indeed cause your death. Understandably, these are situations you might prefer not to think about. However, with high-tech medicine adding weeks, months and sometimes years to our lives (rather than adding "life" to our years), we all run the risk of being incapacitated before we die. This leaves some serious questions for you, and indeed everyone, to ponder and to plan for.

Consider what you would want to happen if a serious accident or illness left you in a situation where:

- you are unable to speak, move, feel or are in constant pain;
- only a respirator and feeding tube are keeping you alive; and
- your quality of life is virtually non-existent and there is no real hope of improvement.

Would you want to stretch your life out on life support, or would you rather let nature take its course? Where would you want to draw the line? When should it end?

Unfortunately, far too many people find themselves in those or similar situations without warning and without the benefit of having asked and answered those questions. These people have no control over the medical care they are receiving. These people have no choice but to "live." You can avoid this if you are practical. Consider your alternatives and make a choice.

If this choice is hard for you to contemplate, think of how it will be for your loved ones if you do nothing. If anything should ever happen to you, they will be the ones who will have to bear the emotional trauma of dealing with your permanent incapacity. They will be the ones that will have to visit you in a hospital and make the tough decisions for you. They will be the ones who must consider how to foot the bill for years of hospital care notwithstanding that there might be no possible chance of recovery for you. They may even end up paying these bills themselves.

We don't mean in this section to scare you, or to convince you whether it's right or wrong to make a living will. Our goal is just to prompt you into thinking about this important matter for yourself. The decision about whether to make a living will is, of course, yours to make.

But having the right to decide what medical treatment you receive, if any, during a terminal illness is what living wills are all about. They allow you to decide these things now, while you can. It is about doing it calmly and without any pressure, and then articulating your wishes in a legal document that will be there to guide your doctors, friends and family if and when you come into the emergency room unable to tell them what you really want.

Keep in mind that a living will does not allow you to appoint another to make life-sustaining decisions for you; that power can only be granted under a healthcare power of attorney. Your agent under a living will typically has powers of enforcement or revocation only.

In addition, although you may have a living will, certain states have legal restrictions and requirements concerning medical treatment that must be adhered to notwithstanding the terms of your living will. For example, some states require that you receive medical treatment for a certain period regardless of your living will. In these states, if you are diagnosed to be in a state of permanent unconsciousness, laws may require that you receive medical treatment for 60 or 90 days before the doctors can make a decision to implement your wishes as stated in your living will. Or if your condition shows zero brain activity, laws may require that you receive medical treatment for a certain number of hours before the terms of your living will can be implemented.

Other legal limitations may also arise. For instance, the provisions in your state may prevent a living will from being implemented if a woman is pregnant and may declare that the living will is ineffective during the pregnancy.

To be certain of the effectiveness and legality of your living will, and learn what provisos state law may apply, it's best to contact a lawyer in your state or ask a relevant government agency for information.

As previously mentioned, some states allow you to name an agent who may either revoke or enforce your living will. It is generally considered that when you name an agent, you are giving that person the power and authority to go to court on your behalf and ask a judge to either revoke or enforce the terms of your living will. However, in some cases, depending on the content of your living will, the agent does not need to go to court, but can merely instruct the medical care providers to either disregard or to enforce your wishes as set out in the living will. Alternatively, the agent may only be able to temporally suspend the operation of your living will so that it is not used at a specific time but may be used later.

Appointing a person to enforce or revoke your healthcare decisions can be useful because it allows for advocacy on your behalf which could help get over difficulties in interpreting your living will. It's also worth remembering that if a physician refuses to respect the terms of your living will, you have the right to be transferred to another physician or hospital that will honor the document. An agent can be especially useful in ensuring that this happens.

Once you have decided to make a living will, you should check the laws that may apply in your state. Many states have specific forms, and a few states have required language that should be included in your living will. When you have determined the laws that apply in your state and what form you need to use, there are a few final steps you should take to ensure that your wishes will be respected when the time comes. Specifically, you should:

- Discuss the terms of your AMD with your doctor before you sign it. Make sure you are both comfortable with what it says. He or she may suggest something you hadn't thought of that you might decide to include.

- Comply with your state's signature and witness requirements. As mentioned, states have various requirements about who can be a witness, how many witnesses are needed, and if the directive must be notarized.

- Provide copies of the signed directive to your doctor and hospital, your agent if one is named, family members, your lawyer, and other significant people in your life.

When you have made your living will or AMD of any kind, it is a good idea to carry a card in your wallet or purse confirming that you have done so. This way, should you be admitted to a medical facility and unable to communicate, healthcare providers will be alerted to the fact that you have set out your requirements in relation to end-of-life treatments and will be legally bound to honor your wishes. By including on your card the contact names and numbers of key family members, details of your doctor, and details of the location of your advance directives if you have any, your healthcare providers will be able to determine your healthcare wishes when most needed.

As you will have no doubt gathered from the foregoing, the principal limitation of living wills is that they only come into play when you are either terminally ill or permanently unconscious and cannot tell your doctors what you want done. It therefore does not apply where, for example, you are unconscious due to a minor accident or illness or where you are suffering from a mental illness. This is where a healthcare power of attorney comes into play.

Most professionals agree that the best approach in dealing with healthcare issues is to have both a living will and a healthcare power of attorney. As already pointed out, using a living will in isolation is problematic as it only relates to end-of-life decisions. As such, to cover all other medical decisions, it always advised to make a healthcare power of attorney as well. It's even better when you can combine both into one document, because it lessens the likelihood of any conflict arising between two separate documents. Fortunately, many states allow you to combine the two documents.

As a practical matter, it's also useful to appoint the same person as your agent under both your living will and healthcare power of attorney. However, the choice is up to you.

Do-Not-Resuscitate Orders

Another type of advance instruction to doctors that should be mentioned is a "do-not-resuscitate," or DNR order. Here the patient is notifying emergency personnel and hospital staff that he or she does not want to be resuscitated if he or she stops breathing. Unlike living wills, a DNR does not simply apply when the patient is suffering from a terminal illness or is in a state of permanent unconsciousness. Rather, a DNR is usually signed when a person is so ill or so old and suffering that they do not wish to have heroic measures used to keep them alive.

A DNR is supposed to be honored by emergency personnel, doctors, and nurses, including the staff of nursing homes. However, sometimes the individual healthcare provider is not comfortable with allowing someone to die under these circumstances. So, this can result in conflicts of interest. In such circumstances, you may wish to include DNR provisions in your living will. That way, you agent can arrange to have you removed to another care facility that will honor your wishes.

Conservatorships and Guardianships

When a person suffers from a mental incapacity rendering him unable to manage his or her own affairs, it is possible to petition the court to have him placed under a conservatorship or guardianship, whereby a person appointed by the court will take care of the incapacitated person's financial affairs and healthcare.

The term "conservator" refers to a person appointed to protect a fully or partially incapacitated person's assets and finances, whereas a "guardian" is responsible for their food, healthcare, housing, medical treatment and so on. In some states, the person who arranges for the care of the incapacitated person is called the "guardian of the person" and the person who is in charge of the money is called the "guardian of the estate." The incapacitated person is called the "conservatee" or the "ward."

A petition for appointment of a conservator and/or guardian is often brought by a concerned relative who believes that the allegedly incapacitated person is making poor decisions. Sometimes, when family members disagree strongly about the medical treatment of an unconscious or gravely ill person, the hospital will ask the court to appoint a guardian to make medical decisions. A durable healthcare power of attorney is intended to avoid the necessity of this procedure. But as an alternative to a power of attorney, some states permit a person to designate the person whom they wish to be appointed as their guardian if one is ever needed.

The petition for appointment of a conservator and/or guardian must be supported by medical affidavits or other sworn statements and may name the person whom the applicant wishes to have appointed. In some states, the petition must include an affidavit from a physician who has recently examined the allegedly incompetent person and determined that he or she, as a medical matter, cannot make rational decisions.

Unfortunately, conservatorship/guardianship court proceedings are often bitter and ruinously expensive family fights. The concerned relative may be one who expects to inherit from the proposed ward and is often more concerned that the allegedly incapacitated person is spending the expected inheritance. If the proposed ward believes that he or she is quite competent to manage his or her affairs, contesting the appointment of a conservator involves challenging the motives of relatives.

The appointment of a conservator and/or guardian requires a determination by the judge that the proposed ward is mentally or physically unable to manage his or her own affairs, including healthcare, in a rational manner. The legal term is that the ward is incompetent.

The court will arrange for a report by a suitable person, who will endeavour to interview the petitioner, their healthcare providers, the person concerned, and other relevant parties. The court may also appoint a doctor to examine and report on the ward's level of incapacity. The ward has rights to consent to or oppose the application or can simply submit to the procedure.

Obviously, whether a person is incompeent or not involves subjective value judgments. People have a right to be foolish with their assets—there's no law against giving all your money to a home for wayward cats—and so this alone should not be the basis for declaring someone incompetent. Usually, a court finds a person to be incompetent when some mental or physical disease distorts the judgement that they would usually exercise. In principle, mere age is not supposed to be a factor, but discrimination against the elderly sometimes occurs.

Once a conservator or guardian is appointed, the court supervises their actions by requiring them to keep detailed records and submit annual accountings. Where a conservator proposes to implement a major transaction, such as sale of the conservatee's house, permission will need to be obtained in advance from the court.

The guardianship/conservatorship procedure may at times be a necessary solution to a painful family situation. However, the procedure affords many opportunities for greed and dishonesty. Although the court is supposed to oversee the administration of incapacitated persons' money, such supervision is often perfunctory at best.

The position of conservator/guardian can be highly profitable. Often, the conservator is a lawyer and he or she promptly hires his or her law firm as counsel. That means that both the conservator/ guardian and the law firm charge for their services. In some states, the conservator is paid a small percentage of every amount that is received by the estate. That gives the conservator a big incentive to buy and sell assets because he or she makes money on every sale.

Control over another person's assets provides a lucrative chance to profit by various underhanded strategies. The sale of a valuable piece of property may look proper on the surface but the conservator may sell the property to a buddy at a low price in exchange for an under the table kickback. Even a careful and honest judge, who is reviewing the transaction, may not realize what has happened.

A conservatorship or guardianship proceeding, of course, may be the only remedy available where the ill or injured party no longer has the legal capacity to create a power of attorney instructing their agent what they want done. It highlights, however, the advantage of a power of attorney, where you can choose who will be your agent, leave binding instructions, and provide for someone to oversee what goes on.

CHAPTER 8

Preparing Your Own Powers of Attorney

Now that you clearly understand the need for a power of attorney (or multiple powers of attorney) and the issues and decisions involved in creating one, it is time to bring together all of the pieces of the puzzle and create your own document(s). In this final chapter, we will take you step-by-step through the process of doing so.

Assess Your Individual Circumstances

Before creating a power of attorney, you will need to determine whether you actually need such a legal document in place at this time, what type (or types) of powers of attorney is most appropriate for you, and who should act as your agent (or agents) to manage certain affairs on your behalf.

To answer those questions, you should take an honest look at your individual circumstances. The factors you should consider include:

- Your age
- Your health
- Your family demographics—e.g. married or single, with dependents or without, etc.
- Your family dynamics
- The size, type, and complexity of your financial affairs
- The location of your assets

- Availability of persons who you trust who could act as agents for both financial and healthcare purposes

- Your current ability to manage your own affairs

Determine Whether You Need a Power of Attorney

As we've discussed throughout the book, it is a good idea for most adults to have both a financial power of attorney and a healthcare power of attorney, even if they are young and do not foresee any need for assistance in managing their affairs for the foreseeable future. Accidents and unforeseen illnesses can happen at any time, and if a catastrophic event leaves you incapacitated, then you put yourself, your assets, and even your family at risk if you have not appointed someone to manage your affairs and make medical decisions on your behalf while you are unable to do so. This is true whether you are young or old, married, or single, with children or without, in good health or poor.

The need and urgency for such powers of attorney increase, sometimes dramatically, depending on the personal assessment you have made. For example, if you are aging, in poor health, work in a dangerous environment, have dependents, require professional assistance in managing your assets, etc., you should make creating the appropriate powers of attorney a top priority in your life before it is too late to do so.

Select the Types of Powers of Attorney that are Best for You

Assuming you have decided to create one or more powers of attorney, the next question is what type or types of power of attorney you should create. As we have previously discussed, the minimum required protection for most people will involve creating two initial powers of attorney:

- a durable general power of attorney appointing a trusted person to manage your financial affairs in the event you become incapacitated; and

- a durable healthcare power of attorney (along with a living will) appointing a trusted person to make medical decisions should you become incapacitated.

After that, your need for additional or different types of powers of attorney will depend on your individual circumstances.

For example, if your financial affairs are diverse and complex, you may want to create two separate limited powers of attorney. The first would grant someone who can oversee and manage more complex transactions a limited financial power of attorney over certain matters such as your investments, and the second would give someone more close to you a financial power of attorney over your more basic, day-to-day financial affairs like paying your bills, collecting salary and benefits, etc.

If you have assets in several different states, you may want to create several powers of attorney appointing agents in those different jurisdictions to manage the properties on your behalf if a standard agency relationship is inadequate. Or if you bank at several institutions that have their own power of attorney forms, you should probably use those forms to create additional powers of attorney so your agent is not blocked from transacting business at those banks.

You may also require immediate assistance with respect to managing your affairs, in which case you would want some or all or your powers of attorney to take effect at the time they are created rather than at a later date.

The bottom line is that you should take a close look at your current or future needs, and make sure that the powers of attorney you create cover all of them without any gaps.

Choose an Agent

Now that you know what types of powers of attorney you need and the purposes they will serve, it is time to choose an agent or agents to carry out those purposes if and when they are required. As we detailed in Chapter 6, there are many factors to consider in choosing an agent, but the main considerations are whether your proposed agent is someone you trust, and whether he or she is capable and available to perform the required tasks and make the required decisions.

It may well be that your spouse, partner, sibling, or best friend can serve all your immediate and long-term requirements for both a financial and healthcare power of attorney. Or you may want to delegate the two functions to two different people—for example, appointing your best friend who is your financial advisor to handle your investments, and your sister to handle medical decisions and day-to-day financial affairs.

In any event, if possible, it is a good idea to select alternate agents for each function who can serve if the initial agent becomes unable or unwilling to perform the required tasks. Remember, just as an unforeseen event can happen to you, it can happen to your agent as well. In addition, it may happen that your agent simply ceases wanting to perform the role. So, having a backup in place is always a good idea.

Finally, have a heart-to-heart conversation with your proposed agents to make sure they understand what is required and what you expect of them, as well as to confirm that they are willing and able to perform the desired role on your behalf.

Create Your Power of Attorney Document

You should now have all the pieces in place that you need to create one or more powers of attorney to suit your needs. As such, the next question is whether you can do so using a form/ kit or whether you need professional advice. Once again, this will probably depend on your individual circumstances, mainly the complexity of your financial and medical affairs, the number and type of powers of attorney you desire, and the level of detail and instructions you wish to include in your documents.

If you want a basic durable general power of attorney and a basic healthcare power of attorney, with the authority of the agent under each commencing at the time of your incapacity, then you can use this book (or any of the other power of attorney kits published by EstateBee) to create your document. Nonetheless, you should still check to make sure your powers of attorney conform to the law of the jurisdictions in which they will be used, and that they are thought through and prepared properly so as not to have any unintended negative consequences.

On the other hand, if your affairs are complex, will require that responsibility for your financial affairs be delegated among more than one agent, involve assets in several jurisdictions, etc., it is probably a good idea to get some professional legal assistance. You can have an attorney prepare the documents for you, or they can ask the relevant questions and review documents you have prepared to make sure they are legally binding and will serve the intended purposes.

In either scenario, you need to think through exactly what you want to accomplish with your powers of attorney and how you want them carried out. Then you need to make sure that any instructions and/or limits you desire are written clearly so that both your agent and any third party reading the power of attorney document will understand precisely its purpose, scope, duration, etc.

Sign and Deliver Your Powers of Attorney

After drafting your power of attorney documents and ensuring that they will serve your purposes and be legally binding under the applicable state laws, it is time to execute and deliver your documents.

The best practice is to have you, your agent, and the witnesses to each power of attorney sign at the same time and in the same place. This is required with respect to you as principal and your witnesses, and desirable with respect to your agent. If your agent is unavailable, at least have him or her sign an acknowledgement when you deliver the document (in some states this is required for the agent's powers to commence). Better still, you and your witnesses should sign your power of attorney in the presence of a notary and have the notary formally notarize the power of attorney. This will help prevent legal challenges to the power of attorney and the authority granted under it.

The next step is to deliver your healthcare power of attorney, and any other advanced medical directive such as a living will, to your medical practitioners and hospital. In addition, it is a good idea to put your financial power of attorney on file with your bank and other financial institutions. Also, you may want to give a copy to certain family members and discuss why and for what purposes you created your powers of attorney, as well as how and why you selected your agents.

Make sure you keep an up-to-date list of everyone who has a copy of your powers of attorney.

Provide Relevant Information to Your Agents

Unless your agent or agents have access to the information needed to perform their roles under your powers of attorney, then appointing them to act on your behalf may be futile. Therefore, you need to provide them with the documents, information, computer files, digital passwords, etc. necessary for them to perform their responsibilities.

If the powers of your agents do not commence until you become incapacitated, and you do not feel comfortable providing them with all of your personal information and passwords beforehand, then you need to put in place some mechanism by which all of this material and access data is given to them immediately after you become incapacitated.

In doing so, you should create a detailed list of all your digital accounts, along with their passwords and security question answers. The importance of preparing and maintaining this inventory cannot be overstated, because it may be impossible for your agents to discover many digital assets if they do not even know these assets exist and where to look for them.

Once you have created such a digital inventory, the next step is to find a secure place to keep this vital information, which could lead to identity theft if obtained by the wrong person. The key is to find a system that meets your strict security requirements and matches your technological capabilities to ensure that you use the system you select. The available methods range from placing the information on a document or flash drive that is kept in your safety deposit box (which your agent should have access to via the power of attorney), to creating a digital account with an online storage service. One place not to put this information is in your will, because after you die this becomes a public document.

Online storage companies offer services to allow users to store digital account information and passwords, as well as documents, using state-of-the-art security for a monthly or yearly fee. Upon your death or incapacity, a person you designate is allowed immediate access to the online storage account and can obtain the digital information they need to manage your affairs. Remember, the information held in the online storage account must be accurate and up to date for the service to work as intended.

Finally, you should provide your agent a road map to your accounts and specific instructions as to how to manage them upon your incapacity. This could be as simple as describing an automatic monthly credit card payment, or as complicated as a web of brokerage and investment accounts with supporting computer files.

Periodically Review Your Power of Attorney Documents and Terms

Finally, you should periodically review your powers of attorney to make sure that a change in circumstances does not require you to revoke or modify your existing powers of attorney, or to create additional powers of attorney. For example, if any agent or alternate agent you have named is no longer available or is no longer an appropriate person to manage your affairs or make decisions on your behalf, then you will need to designate a new agent. Or if you have purchased assets in new jurisdictions, you may need additional powers of attorney to cover those jurisdictions.

Conclusion

With the comfort of knowing that you have the appropriate powers of attorney in place, that they have been properly prepared, and that your most trusted family members, friends and/or advisors will be managing your financial affairs and making medical decisions on your behalf should anything catastrophic occur, you can now relax and enjoy today—and every day thereafter.

EstateBee is proud to have assisted you in this endeavor.

Please see some of our other publications, such as "Estate Planning Essentials", to receive the same high standard of information and assistance in other areas.

Resource

EstateBee's **Estate Planning Essentials** introduces you to some of the devices used in estate planning such as wills, trusts, powers of attorney, medical directives, transfer on death accounts and more. Particular attention is paid throughout to beneficiaries, children, disinheritance, incapacity, and taxes. You will learn everything necessary to enable you to put an effective estate plan in place, without the need or cost of lawyers.

Get your copy at

www.estate-bee.com/product/estate-planning-essentials/

Appendices

Appendix 1

Make Your Own Power of Attorney

Ok, now that you understand what a power of attorney is, how it operates in practice and the importance of having one, it is time for you to consider making your own. At the back of this book, we have included several different types of power of attorney forms (all of which we discussed in this book). A brief description of each form is set out below.

General Power of Attorney

- Covers the whole cross section of your legal and financial affairs.
- Agent's authority commences on signing.
- Agent's authority terminates (i) when you revoke your agent's authority, (ii) on your incapacity or (iii) on your death. You could also amend the document to state that the authority of your agent will end at a specific time or on the occurrence of a specific event.

Durable General Power of Attorney

- Covers the whole cross section of your legal and financial affairs.
- Agent's authority commences either on signing or following a medical determination that you have become incapacitated.
- Agent's authority terminates (i) when you revoke the agent's authority, or (ii) on your death. You could also amend the document to state that the authority of your agent will end at a specific time or on the occurrence of a specific event.
- Not terminated by incapacity and operates during any period in which you are incapacitated.

Limited Power of Attorney

- Has limited scope and only covers a limited section of your legal and financial affairs. You are free to choose the scope of your agent's authority.
- Agent's authority commences on signing.
- Agent's authority terminates (i) when you revoke your agent's authority, (ii) on your incapacity, (iii) on your death, (iv) on a specific date or (v) on the occurrence of a specific event.

Durable Limited Power of Attorney

- Has limited scope and only covers a limited section of your legal and financial affairs. You are free to choose the scope of your agent's authority.

- Agent's authority commences either on signing or following a medical determination that you have become incapacitated.

- Agent's authority terminates (i) when you revoke your agent's authority, (ii) on your death, (iii) on a specific date or (iv) on the occurrence of a specific event.

- Not terminated by incapacity and operates during any period in which you are incapacitated.

Durable Power of Attorney for Healthcare and Living Will

- Has wide scope and covers your healthcare and medical affairs. You are free to choose the scope of your agent's authority and to direct your agent regarding your preferred medical treatment.

- Also includes details of your wishes regarding end-of-life medical treatment.

- Agent's authority only commences following a medical determination that you have become incapacitated.

- Agent's authority terminates (i) when you revoke the agent's authority, or (ii) on your death. You could also amend the document to state that the authority of your agent will end at a specific time or on the occurrence of a specific event.

- Not terminated by incapacity and operates during any period in which you are incapacitated.

In addition to the above documents, we have also included several other useful documents at the back of this book including a Notice of Revocation of a Power of Attorney and an Agent's Acceptance of Appointment.

Before deciding to use any of the forms attached to this book, you should carefully review the forms to ensure that they meet your requirements and are suitable having regard to your circumstances. If you are in any doubt as to the suitability of the documents for your use or the scope of the documents, you should consult an attorney before using these documents.

Where you decide to use any of the above-mentioned documents, be sure to read the document in full and follow the signing instructions carefully. Remember, these documents are provided on an 'as-is' basis and the decision to use them is yours.

Appendix 2

Signing Instructions

Instructions for Completion of the General Power of Attorney

1. Carefully read all the instructions below.

2. Print out the document and complete it neatly using a pen or carefully edit the text version of the form (that is available to you to downlad) on your computer.

3. On the cover page of the document, insert the date of execution of the power of attorney as well as your name, as principal, in the spaces provided.

4. Clause 1 identifies the parties to the power of attorney. In this clause, you will need to enter (i) your name and address, (ii) that of your primary agent and (iii) that of your alternate agent in the spaces provided.

5. In clause 12, enter your state of residence.

6. If you wish to use a notary, arrange to meet with a notary. Once you meet the notary, you should proceed to step 7 – in the notary's presence. If you do not wish to use a notary, then simply go to step 7 and disregard references to the notary.

7. In the execution block, immediately after clause 12, enter the date, month, year, and place of execution. Then sign your name on the signature line above the words "The Principal" in the presence of the notary and two witnesses.

   Your witnesses should not be a person who is:

   - your agent or attorney-in-fact.
   - the notary acknowledging your signature.
   - a relation by blood, marriage, or adoption to you or your agent; or a spouse of any such person.
   - financially responsible for your medical care.
   - entitled to any portion of your estate following your death.
   - a beneficiary under an insurance policy on your life.
   - entitled to make claim against your estate (such as creditors).
   - your attending physician, nor an employee of such a physician.

8. You should have the two witnesses who witnessed your execution of the power of attorney complete the "Witness Affidavit" section of the document.

9. You should then have a notary complete the "Notary Affidavit" section of the document.

10. If you intend to register your document in the Registry of Deeds in Illinois, Indiana, Kentucky, or Minnesota you will need to complete the "Preparation Statement" section of the document. This section simply identifies the person who has prepared the document. In most cases, this will be you (the principal). However, if someone has prepared it on your behalf, they should be

identified in this section.

11. If you live in California, Georgia, Montana, New Hampshire, Pennsylvania, Vermont, or Wisconsin you will need to have your agent accept his or her appointment under the power of attorney before they can lawfully act. You can do this by having your agent complete and sign the Acknowledgement of Agent section of the document.

In fact, while there is no obligation to do so, it is both recommended and good practice to always get your agent to sign this acknowledgement irrespective of what state you reside it.

12. If your power of attorney is to grant authority over real property to your agent, it should also be registered in the registry of deeds your agent may not be deemed to have authority to deal with your real property.

When you register the document is largely up to you as there are generally no time requirements for registration. If it is not needed straight away, and you do not want the document placed on public record straight away, you can hold off on registering it until it is needed. When the time comes, your agent can then register it. However, if you are adopting this approach, you need to check with the clerk in the registry of deeds to see what the specific requirements are for registering. For example, in some states, the documents must be a specific size or on specific types of paper. If your document meets the required standards, you can then choose to wait before registering.

Instructions for Completion of the Durable General Power of Attorney

1. Carefully read all the instructions below.

2. Print out the document and complete it neatly using a pen or carefully edit the text version of the form (that is available to you to download) on your computer.

3. On the cover page of the document, insert the date of execution of the power of attorney as well as your name, as principal, in the spaces provided.

4. Clause 1 identifies the parties to the power of attorney. In this clause, you will need to enter (i) your name and address, (ii) that of your primary agent and (iii) that of your alternate agent in the spaces provided.

5. In clause 3, you will need to decide whether you would like your power of attorney to (i) take effect immediately, in which case your agent can immediately commence acting for you; or (ii) only come into effect when you are deemed to be mentally incapacitated by a doctor. If you would prefer option (i), then initial the first paragraph of this clause in the space provided. If you would prefer option (ii), then initial the second paragraph of this clause in the space provided.

    If you select option (ii) and initial the second paragraph, you will also need to add the name and address of a physician in the third paragraph. This will be the physician that you would prefer to have examine you to determine whether you are mentally incapacitated.

6. In clause 12, enter your state of residence.

7. If you wish to use a notary, arrange to meet with a notary. Once you meet the notary, you should proceed to step 8 – in the notary's presence. If you do not wish to use a notary, then simply go to step 8 and disregard references to the notary.

8. In the execution block, immediately after clause 12, enter the date, month, year, and place of execution. Then sign your name on the signature line above the words "The Principal" in the presence of the notary and two witnesses.

    Your witnesses should not be a person who is:

    *   your agent or attorney-in-fact.

    *   the notary acknowledging your signature.

    *   a relation by blood, marriage, or adoption to you or your agent; or a spouse of any such person.

    *   financially responsible for your medical care.

    *   entitled to any portion of your estate following your death.

    *   a beneficiary under an insurance policy on your life.

    *   entitled to make claim against your estate (such as creditors).

- your attending physician, nor an employee of such a physician.

9. You should have the two witnesses who witnessed your execution of the power of attorney complete the "Witness Affidavit" section of the document.

10. You should then have a notary complete the "Notary Affidavit" section of the document.

11. If you intend to register your document in the Registry of Deeds in Illinois, Indiana, Kentucky, or Minnesota you will need to complete the "Preparation Statement" section of the document. This section simply identifies the person who has prepared the document. In most cases, this will be you (the principal). However, if someone has prepared it on your behalf, they should be identified in this section.

12. If you live in California, Georgia, Montana, New Hampshire, Pennsylvania, Vermont, or Wisconsin you will need to have your agent accept his or her appointment under the power of attorney before they can lawfully act. You can do this by having your agent complete and sign the Acknowledgement of Agent section of the document.

    In fact, while there is no obligation to do so, it is both recommended and good practice to always get your agent to sign this acknowledgement irrespective of what state you reside it.

    In Georgia, you will also need to have your agent complete the Agent's Acceptance of Appointment document in Appendix 4 and attach it to your Power of Attorney document.

13. If you are making a power of attorney for use in either North Carolina or South Carolina, then you must record it with the registry of deeds before it can be deemed to be durable. Similarly, if your power of attorney is to grant authority over real property to your agent, it should also be registered in the registry of deeds, otherwise your agent may not be deemed to have authority to deal with your real property.

    When you register the document is largely up to you as there are generally no time requirements for registration. If it is not needed straight away, and you do not want the document placed on public record straight away, you can hold off on registering it until it is needed. When the time comes, your agent can then register it. However, if you are adopting this approach, you need to check with the clerk in the registry of deeds to see what the specific requirements are for registering. For example, in some states, the documents must be a specific size or on specific types of paper. If your document meets the required standards, you can then choose to wait before registering.

Instructions for Completion of the Limited Power of Attorney

1. Carefully read all the instructions below.

2. Print out the document and complete it neatly using a pen or carefully edit the text version of the form (that is available to you to downlad) on your computer.

3. On the cover page of the document, insert the date of execution of the power of attorney as well as your name, as principal, in the spaces provided.

4. Clause 1 identifies the parties to the power of attorney. In this clause, you will need to enter (i) your name and address, (ii) that of your primary agent and (iii) that of your alternate agent in the spaces provided.

5. In clause 2, specify the maximum duration for which your agent will be entitled to act on your behalf under the Power of Attorney.

6. In clause 4, specify the purpose(s) for which the power of attorney is being granted. E.g. "carrying out real estate transactions" or "purchasing a detached office property located at 123 Little Street, Small town for the sum of $250,000 from John Smith". Be as specific and concise as possible.

7. In clause 11, enter your state of residence.

8. If you wish to use a notary, arrange to meet with a notary. Once you meet the notary, you should proceed to step 9 – in the notary's presence. If you do not wish to use a notary, then simply go to step 9 and disregard references to the notary.

9. In the execution block, immediately after clause 11, enter the date, month, year, and place of execution. Then sign your name on the signature line above the words "The Principal" in the presence of the notary and two witnesses.

   Your witnesses should not be a person who is:

   - your agent or attorney-in-fact.
   - the notary acknowledging your signature.
   - a relation by blood, marriage, or adoption to you or your agent; or a spouse of any such person.
   - financially responsible for your medical care.
   - entitled to any portion of your estate following your death.
   - a beneficiary under an insurance policy on your life.
   - entitled to make claim against your estate (such as creditors).
   - your attending physician, nor an employee of such a physician.

10. You should have the two witnesses who witnessed your execution of the power of attorney

complete the "Witness Affidavit" section of the document.

11. You should then have a notary complete the "Notary Affidavit" section of the document.

12. If you intend to register your document in the Registry of Deeds in Illinois, Indiana, Kentucky, or Minnesota you will need to complete the "Preparation Statement" section of the document. This section simply identifies the person who has prepared the document. In most cases, this will be you (the principal). However, if someone has prepared it on your behalf, they should be identified in this section.

13. If you live in California, Georgia, Montana, New Hampshire, Pennsylvania, Vermont, or Wisconsin you will need to have your agent accept his or her appointment under the power of attorney before they can lawfully act. You can do this by having your agent complete and sign the Acknowledgement of Agent section of the document.

    In fact, while there is no obligation to do so, it is both recommended and good practice to always get your agent to sign this acknowledgement irrespective of what state you reside it.

14. If your power of attorney is to grant authority over real property to your agent, it should also be registered in the registry of deeds your agent may not be deemed to have authority to deal with your real property.

    When you register the document is largely up to you as there are generally no time requirements for registration. If it is not needed straight away, and you do not want the document placed on public record straight away, you can hold off on registering it until it is needed. When the time comes, your agent can then register it. However, if you are adopting this approach, you need to check with the clerk in the registry of deeds to see what the specific requirements are for registering. For example, in some states, the documents must be a specific size or on specific types of paper. If your document meets the required standards, you can then choose to wait before registering.

Instructions for Completion of the Durable Limited Power of Attorney

1.   Carefully read all the instructions below.

2.   Print out the document and complete it neatly using a pen or carefully edit the text version of the form (that is available to you to download) on your computer.

3.   On the cover page of the document, insert the date of execution of the power of attorney as well as your name, as principal, in the spaces provided.

4.   Clause 1 identifies the parties to the power of attorney. In this clause, you will need to enter (i) your name and address, (ii) that of your primary agent and (iii) that of your alternate agent in the spaces provided.

5.   In clause 2, specify the maximum duration for which your agent will be entitled to act on your behalf under the Power of Attorney.

6.   In clause 3, you will need to decide whether you would like your power of attorney to (i) take effect immediately, in which case your agent can immediately commence acting for you; or (ii) only come into effect when you are deemed to be mentally incapacitated by a doctor. If you would prefer option (i), then initial the first paragraph of this clause in the space provided. If you would prefer option (ii), then initial the second paragraph of this clause in the space provided.

      If you select option (ii) and initial the second paragraph, you will also need to add the name and address of a physician in the third paragraph. This will be the physician that you would prefer to have examine you to determine whether you are mentally incapacitated.

7.   In clause 4, specify the purpose(s) for which the power of attorney is being granted. E.g. "carrying out real estate transactions" or "purchasing a detached office property located at 123 Little Street, Small town for the sum of $250,000 from John Smith". Be as specific and concise as possible.

8.   In clause 11, enter your state of residence.

9.   If you wish to use a notary, arrange to meet with a notary. Once you meet the notary, you should proceed to step 10 – in the notary's presence. If you do not wish to use a notary, then simply go to step 10 and disregard references to the notary.

10.   In the execution block, immediately after clause 12, enter the date, month, year, and place of execution. Then sign your name on the signature line above the words "The Principal" in the presence of the notary and two witnesses.

      Your witnesses should not be a person who is:

      ● your agent or attorney-in-fact.

      ● the notary acknowledging your signature.

- a relation by blood, marriage, or adoption to you or your agent; or a spouse of any such person.

- financially responsible for your medical care.

- entitled to any portion of your estate following your death.

- a beneficiary under an insurance policy on your life.

- entitled to make claim against your estate (such as creditors).

- your attending physician, nor an employee of such a physician.

11. You should have the two witnesses who witnessed your execution of the power of attorney complete the "Witness Affidavit" section of the document.

12. You should then have a notary complete the "Notary Affidavit" section of the document.

13. If you intend to register your document in the Registry of Deeds in Illinois, Indiana, Kentucky, or Minnesota you will need to complete the "Preparation Statement" section of the document. This section simply identifies the person who has prepared the document. In most cases, this will be you (the principal). However, if someone has prepared it on your behalf, they should be identified in this section.

14. If you live in California, Georgia, Montana, New Hampshire, Pennsylvania, Vermont, or Wisconsin you will need to have your agent accept his or her appointment under the power of attorney before they can lawfully act. You can do this by having your agent complete and sign the Acknowledgement of Agent section of the document.

    In fact, while there is no obligation to do so, it is both recommended and good practice to always get your agent to sign this acknowledgement irrespective of what state you reside it.

    In Georgia, you will also need to have your agent complete the Agent's Acceptance of Appointment document in Appendix 4 and attach it to your Power of Attorney document.

15. If you are making a power of attorney for use in either North Carolina or South Carolina, then you must record it with the registry of deeds before it can be deemed to be durable. Similarly, if your power of attorney is to grant authority over real property to your agent, it should also be registered in the registry of deeds, otherwise your agent may not be deemed to have authority to deal with your real property.

    When you register the document is largely up to you as there are generally no time requirements for registration. If it is not needed straight away, and you do not want the document placed on public record straight away, you can hold off on registering it until it is needed. When the time comes, your agent can then register it. However, if you are adopting this approach, you need to check with the clerk in the registry of deeds to see what the specific requirements are for registering. For example, in some states, the documents must be a specific size or on specific types of paper. If your document meets the required standards, you can then choose to wait before registering.

Instructions for Completion of the Agent's Acceptance of Appointment

1. Carefully read all the instructions below.

2. Print out the document and complete it neatly using a pen or carefully edit the text version of the form (that is available to you to download) on your computer.

3. The first paragraph identifies the agent and the principal. Therefore, in this paragraph, you will need to enter (i) the name of your agent and (ii) that of the principal in the spaces provided. Your agent will then need to date and sign the document at the bottom of the page, as well as specify his address.

4. If the power of attorney document grants the agent authority to deal with real estate, the agent should sign the document in front of a notary.

Instructions for Completion of the Durable Power of Attorney for Healthcare & Living Will

1. Carefully read all the instructions below.

2. Print out the document which you intend using and complete it neatly using a pen or carefully edit the text version of the form (that is available to you to download) on your computer.

3. On the cover page of the document, insert the date of execution of the power of attorney as well as your name, as principal, in the spaces provided.

4. The first paragraph of the document identifies the person making the document. In this paragraph, you will need to enter (i) your name and address and (ii) the state in which you reside.

5. In clause 1.1, enter the name, address, home telephone number and work telephone number of your primary agent in the spaces provided.

6. In clause 1.2, enter the name, address, home telephone number and work telephone number of your alternate agent in the spaces provided.

7. In clause 1.2, enter the name, address, home telephone number and work telephone number of your second alternate agent in the spaces provided.

8. In clause 2.1, you are asked to initial one of the two choices available in each of sub-clauses (i) to (iv). Simply insert your initials in the space provided opposite each of the choices you wish to select. Read each of the choices carefully before initialing your preferences.

9. In clause 2.1(v), you can insert any further instructions you wish. If you insert any instructions, you will need to initial the space opposite where you have included your instructions.

10. In clause 6.1, you can specify your end-of-life wishes. The sections are divided into three parts namely (i) terminal conditions, (ii) permanent consciousness, and (iii) maximum treatment. You can either choose to receive the maximum treatment possible in all respects under part (iii) or you can choose to receive or not to receive treatment subject to a few exceptions under parts (i) and (ii). You can choose to complete part (iii) alone or parts (i) and (ii) together. You must choose one or the other of these two options (assuming you wish to complete this part of the document).

Once you have decided what options you wish to select, sign your initials beside your chosen options. If you have chosen options (i) and (ii), then you will need to specify whether you want treatment applied or withheld in each case. If you wish to have treatment applied, you should place your initials beside the word "shall". If you wish to have treatment withheld, you should place your initials beside the words "shall not". Once you have done this, you should place your initials beside any specific treatments that you want to receive. If you do not want to receive a specific treatment, do not place your initials beside that treatment.

11. In clause 7, please select your preference for the administration of treatment for the relief of pain. Please initial once choice only.

12. In clause 8, if you are female, please indicate whether your preferences in relation to end-of-life treatment should continue to apply if you are pregnant. Please initial once choice only.

13. In clause 9.1, please indicate whether you would like to donate your organs following your death. You have three choices – give no organs, give any organs needed or specify your gift in your own words. Please initial one choice only. If you choose to specify your gift in your own words, make sure to complete the section as concisely as possible.

14. If you have decided to gift any organs under clause 9.1, you will also need to complete clause 9.2. In clause 9.2, you can specify the purposes for which you are donating your organs. Please sign your initials beside the purposes for which you are donating your organs. You can choose as many preferences as you wish.

15. In clause 10, you will need to insert details of your primary physician. Your primary physician will have primary responsibility for determining whether you are suffering from a terminal condition or are in a state of permanent unconsciousness. In this clause, you should specify the name, address, and telephone number of your primary physician in the spaces provided. You should also specify the name, address, and telephone number of your alternate physician in the spaces provided.

16. Arrange to meet with a notary. Once you meet the notary, you should proceed to step 17 – in the notary's presence.

17. In the execution block, immediately after clause 11, enter the date, month, year, place, and state of execution. Then sign your name on the signature line above the words "Signature of Principal" in the presence of the notary and two witnesses.

Your witnesses should not be a person who is:

- your agent or attorney-in-fact.
- the notary acknowledging your signature.
- a relation by blood, marriage, or adoption to you or your agent; or a spouse of any such person.
- financially responsible for your medical care.
- entitled to any portion of your estate following your death.
- a beneficiary under an insurance policy on your life.
- entitled to make claim against your estate (such as creditors).
- your attending physician, nor an employee of such a physician.

18. You should have the two witnesses who witnessed your execution of the power of attorney complete the "Witness Affidavit" section of the document.

19. You should then have a notary complete the "Notary Affidavit" section of the document.

Instructions for Completion of the Notice of Revocation of a Power of Attorney

1. Carefully read all the instructions below.

2. Print out the document which you intend using and complete it neatly using a pen or carefully edit the text version of the form (that is available to you to download) on your computer.

3. On the cover page of the document, insert the date of execution of the notice of revocation as well as your name, as principal, in the spaces provided.

4. The first paragraph of the document identifies the parties to the original power of attorney and its date. In this paragraph, you will need to enter (i) your name and address, (ii) the date of the power of attorney and (iii) the name of your agent.

5. Arrange to meet with a notary. Once you meet the notary, you should proceed to step 6 – in the notary's presence.

6. In the execution block, enter the date, month, year, and place of execution. Then sign your name on the signature line above the words "The Principal" in the presence of the notary and two witnesses.

   Your witnesses should not be a person who is:

   - your agent or attorney-in-fact.
   - the notary acknowledging your signature.
   - a relation by blood, marriage, or adoption to you or your agent; or a spouse of any such person.
   - financially responsible for your medical care.
   - entitled to any portion of your estate following your death.
   - a beneficiary under an insurance policy on your life.
   - entitled to make claim against your estate (such as creditors).
   - your attending physician, nor an employee of such a physician.

7. You should have the two witnesses who witnessed your execution of the notice of revocation complete the "Witness Affidavit" section of the document.

8. You should then have a notary complete the "Notary Affidavit" section of the document.

Note: It is not legally required to have a notary witness the execution of your notice of revocation. So, you can dispense with this step if you wish – although you should still have your signature witnessed by two witnesses. It is, however, good practice to have your notice of revocation notarized as it helps prevent a successful challenge to its authenticity.

Appendix 3

Sample Powers of Attorney for Finance and Property

General Power of Attorney for Finance and Property

Downloadable Forms

Blank copies of all this form can be downloaded from the EstateBee website. Simply login to your account or, if you don't have an account, you can create one for free.

www.estate-bee.com/login

Once logged in, go to your profile page and enter the code listed below in the 'Use Codes' tab:

GPOAB1629

Dated this _____ day of _____, 20____

_____

General Power of Attorney
of

_____

(Principal)

Notice: The powers granted by this document are broad and sweeping. If you have any questions about these powers, obtain competent legal advice. This document does not authorize anyone to make medical and other healthcare decisions for you. You may revoke this power of attorney if you later wish to do so provided you are of sound mind.

General Power of Attorney

1. I, _____ of _____ aged eighteen years and upwards hereby appoint _____ of _____ _ as my lawfully appointed attorney in fact (referred to as my "Agent") on and subject to the terms and conditions set out below. If for any reason this person shall be unable or unwilling to act as my Agent, I hereby appoint _____ of _____ _____ to act as my Agent instead subject to the terms and conditions set out herein.

2. This power of attorney shall apply for financial and property applications only and shall remain effective until my incapacity, death, or until revoked by me in writing.

3. This power of attorney shall become and is hereby effective immediately and will continue in full force and effect until terminated in accordance with the provisions of Clause 2. This power of attorney shall, for the avoidance of doubt, be construed as a general power of attorney.

4. I hereby grant (subject to the provisions of Clause 6) my Agent full power and authority over all my finances and property, both real and personal, and authorize my Agent to do and perform each and every act which I could do or perform and I hereby ratify and confirm all that my Agent shall do or cause to be done under this Power of Attorney.

5. Without prejudice to the provisions of Clause 4 but subject always to the provisions of Clause 6, my Agent's powers shall include, but shall not be limited to, the power to:

   (a)   **Real property transactions**

   receive from any person, to retain and to invest and reinvest in any kind of property or investment; to dispose of any property or any interest therein at such times and upon such terms and conditions as shall seem proper and to give good and sufficient instruments of transfer and to receive the proceeds of any such disposition; to purchase, manage, maintain and insure any property and to lease the same for such periods and on such terms as shall seem advantageous, and if advisable to pay for the value of any improvements made by a tenant under any such lease; to incur, extend or renew mortgage indebtedness; to make ordinary and extraordinary repairs and alterations to any building, to raze or erect buildings and to make improvements or to abandon any buildings or property; and to make any agreement of partition of such property and to give or receive money or other property in connection therewith;

   (b)   **Personal property transactions**

   buy, sell, mortgage, hypothecate, assign, transfer, grant options over and deal with all my personal property, tangible or intangible; and to manage, improve, repair and lease same; and to make, do, and transact all and every kind of business of whatever nature in respect thereto; and in each case in such manner and on such terms as my agent deems proper;

(c)   **Commercial transactions**

manage, sell, administer, liquidate, continue, discontinue or otherwise deal with any corporation, partnership or other business interest of mine as my Agent deems fit; to engage, compensate and discharge employees, agents, professional advisors and consultants; to assent to, oppose and participate in any reorganization, recapitalization, merger, consolidation or similar proceeding, to deposit securities, delegate discretionary powers, pay assessments or other expenses and exchange property, all as fully as might be done by persons owning similar property in their own right;

(d)   **Financial transactions**

open, administer, manage and close bank, savings, loans brokerage, and other such accounts in my name, to lodge proceeds to and withdraw proceeds from such accounts, to receive, draw, endorse and sign checks, bank drafts, bills of exchange, loan notes, promissory notes, letters of credit and certificates of deposit in relation to any such account and the proceeds therein; to pay any sums owing in respect of any such account, to use all credit cards issued in my name; to borrow such sums of money as my Agent may from time to time deem fit and to secure any such obligations by mortgage or pledge and to execute all documents in connection therewith;

(e)   **Financial securities**

purchase, exercise, surrender, transfer, sell or otherwise dispose of all rights, options, powers and privileges, and to vote in person or by proxy, in relation to any stocks, bonds or other securities, all as fully as might be done by persons owning similar property in their own right;

(f)   **Commodity and option transactions**

buy, sell, transfer and deal in commodities and options of all types; and to exercise all powers and do all matters and things incidental to the same;

(g)   **Insurance and annuity transactions**

exercise or perform any act or do any thing in connection with any insurance cover I may have in my name (including, but not limited to, taking out new cover, paying premiums, making claims, extending cover, renewing polices and terminating policies) which my Agent deems necessary or prudent to maintain the value of my real or personal property;

(h)   **Estate and trust transactions**

demand, sue for, collect, and receive all legacies, bequests, and gifts due, payable or belonging to me, and take all lawful means, for the recovery thereof and to compromise the same and give discharges for the same; and to transfer any interest I may have in property, whether real or personal, tangible or intangible, to the trustee of any trust that I have created for my benefit;

(i)   **Retirement plans**

create and contribute to any type of retirement plan established in my name or for my benefit; to select any payment option under any retirement plan in which I am a participant or change options I have selected; to make voluntary contributions to such plans; to "roll-over" plan benefits into other retirement plans; to borrow money and purchase assets therefrom and sell assets thereto, if authorized by any such plan; to receive benefits from and engage in transactions (including the making of any plan election) with any retirement plan of which I am a beneficiary, and to exercise all powers necessary or desirable in connection with the maintenance and administration of such plans;

(j)   **Family maintenance**

do all things and acts to maintain and support my family, including the making of any payments to and on behalf of my family that my Agent reasonably deems fit; and to hire accountants, attorneys at law, consultants, clerks, physicians, nurses, agents, servants, workmen, and others and to remove them, and to appoint others in their place, and to pay and allow the persons so employed such salaries, wages, or other remunerations, as my Agent shall deem proper;

(k)   **Benefits**

prepare, execute and file any application or claim for any government, insurance, medical, military or social security benefit that I may be entitled to receive, to receive personal, confidential and medical information; to settle, compromise or contest any related assessments made against me; and to represent me in all matters relating to same;

(l)   **Claims and litigation**

initiate, discontinue, defend and settle all actions, demands, claims and legal proceedings, by arbitration or otherwise, in connection with any or all of my real and personal property and any rights, interests or entitlements that I may have or any matters in which I am in any way concerned, in such manner as my Agent shall deem fit; and to give appropriate discharges, releases and receipt for the same;

(m)   **Taxation**

prepare, execute and file any and all tax and informational returns that I may be entitled or required to make; to pay any taxes, surcharges and penalties duly owing by me, to file claims for tax refunds of every description; to settle, compromise or contest any tax assessments made against me; and to represent me in all matters before the Internal Revenue Service;

(n)   **Safe deposit box**

access any safety deposit box registered in my name alone or jointly with others, and to remove any property or papers located therein; and

(o)   **Deal with contracts**

enter into, negotiate, alter, amend, revoke, and exercise all rights granted under contracts of all types.

6. My Agent shall have no authority to give any of my property to, or to use any of my property for the benefit of, himself or herself. In addition, my agent (i) cannot execute a will, a codicil, or any will substitute on my behalf; (ii) cannot change the beneficiary on any life insurance policy that I own; (iii) cannot make gifts on my behalf; (iv) may not exercise any powers that would cause any assets of mine to be considered taxable to my agent or to my agent's estate for purposes of any income, estate, or inheritance tax, and (v) cannot contravene any medical or healthcare power of attorney or living will I have executed whether prior or subsequent to the execution of this Power of Attorney.

7. The powers conferred on my Agent herein may be exercised by my Agent alone, and my Agent's signature or act under the authority granted herein may be accepted by any third person or organization as fully authorized by me and with the same legal force and effect as if I were personally present, competent and acting on my own behalf.

8. Third parties may rely upon the representations of the Agent as to all matters regarding powers granted to the Agent. No person who acts in reliance on the authority granted under this Power of Attorney shall incur any liability to me or to my estate for permitting the Agent to exercise any power prior to actual knowledge that the Power of Attorney has been revoked or terminated by operation of law or otherwise.

9. No agent named or substituted in this Power of Attorney shall incur any liability to me for acting or refraining from acting under this power, except for such agent's own misconduct, fraud or negligence.

10. My Agent shall provide an accounting for all funds and assets handled and all acts performed as my Agent, if I so request or if such a request is made by any authorized personal representative or fiduciary properly acting on my behalf. My Agent shall not however be obliged to file any such accountings or any inventory with a court and any obligation in this respect is hereby waived to the fullest extent permitted by law.

11. My Agent shall be reimbursed for reasonable expenses incurred while acting as my Agent and may receive reasonable compensation for acting as Agent.

12. This power of attorney will be governed by the laws of the State of _____ without regard for conflicts of laws principles and is intended to be valid in all jurisdictions of the United States of America and all foreign nations.

Executed this _____ day of _____, 20_____, at

_____

_____

_____

The Principal

Witness Affidavit

I declare, on the basis of information and belief, that the person who signed or acknowledged this document (the principal) is personally known to me, that he/she signed or acknowledged this Power of Attorney in my presence, and that he/she appears to be of sound mind and under no duress, fraud, or undue influence. I am not related to the principal by blood, marriage, or adoption, either as a spouse, a lineal ancestor, descendant of the parents of the principal, or spouse of any of them. I am not directly financially responsible for the principal's medical care. I am not entitled to any portion of the principal's estate upon his/her decease, whether under any Will or as an heir by intestate succession, nor am I the beneficiary of an insurance policy on the principal's life, nor do I have a claim against the principal's estate as of this time. I am not the principal's attending physician, nor an employee of the attending physician. No more than one witness is an employee of a health facility in which the principal is a patient. I am not appointed as Healthcare Agent or Successor Healthcare Agent by this document.

Witness No. 1

Signature: _____

Date: _____

Print Name: _____

Telephone: _____

Residence Address: _____

_____

_____

_____

Witness No. 2

Signature: _____

Date: _____

Print Name: _____

Telephone: _____

Residence Address: _____

_____

_____

_____

Notary Affidavit

State of _____   County of _____

On _____ before me, _____, a notary public, personally appeared _____, who proved to me on the basis of satisfactory evidence to be the person whose name is subscribed to the within instrument and acknowledged to me that he/she executed the same in his/her authorized capacity, and that by his/her signature on the instrument he/she executed the instrument. I certify under PENALTY OF PERJURY that the foregoing is true and correct. Witness my hand and official seal.

Signature: _____

Print Name: _____

My commission expires on: _____

(Seal)

Preparation Statement

This document was prepared by the following individual:

_____

Print Name

_____

Signature

Acknowledgment of Agent

By accepting or acting under the appointment, the agent assumes the fiduciary and other legal responsibilities of an agent.

_____

Print Name of Agent

_____

Signature of Agent

Durable General Power of Attorney For Finance and Property

Downloadable Forms

Blank copies of all this form can be downloaded from the EstateBee website. Simply login to your account or, if you don't have an account, you can create one for free.

www.estate-bee.com/login

Once logged in, go to your profile page and enter the code listed below in the 'Use Codes' tab:

DGPOAB1629

Dated this _____ day of _____, 20____

_____

Durable General Power of Attorney

of

_____

(Principal)

> **Notice:** The powers granted by this document are broad and sweeping. If you have any questions about these powers, obtain competent legal advice. This document does not authorize anyone to make medical and other healthcare decisions for you. You may revoke this power of attorney if you later wish to do so provided you are of sound mind.

www.estate-bee.com

Durable General Power of Attorney

1. I, _____ of _____ aged
    eighteen years and upwards hereby appoint _____ of _____
    _____ as my lawfully appointed attorney in fact (referred to as the "Agent") on and subject
    to the terms and conditions set out below. If for any reason this person shall be unable or
    unwilling to act as my Agent, I hereby appoint _____ of _____
    _____ to act as my Agent instead subject to the terms and conditions set out herein.

2. This durable power of attorney shall apply for financial and property applications only and
    shall not be affected by my subsequent disability or incapacity; and, once effective, shall
    remain effective until my death, or until revoked by me in writing.

3. I direct that this durable power of attorney shall become effective in the manner that I have
    expressed below: -

    (initial only one option below)

    _____   This durable power of attorney is hereby effective immediately and shall continue in
    full force and effect until it is revoked or until my death. This power of attorney shall
    be construed as a durable general power of attorney and shall continue to be effective
    even if I become disabled, incapacitated, or incompetent.

    _____   This durable power of attorney shall become effective only in the event that I become
    mentally incapacitated or disabled so that as a result I am not able to manage my
    financial affairs in which case it shall become effective as of the date of the written
    statement to be provided by a physician pursuant to the terms of this Clause 3. If this
    power of attorney becomes effective, it shall remain effective during any period in
    which I am incapacitated or disabled until my death, or until revoked by me in writing
    during a subsequent period of lucidity or non-incapacitation.

    The determination of whether I have become incapacitated or disabled so that I am not
    able to manage my financial affairs shall be made in writing by a licensed physician; if
    practical, this physician shall be _____ of _____
    _or failing him/her any licensed physician having been at least ten years in practice.

    In the event that a licensed physician has made a written determination pursuant
    to this Clause 3 that I have become incapacitated or disabled and as a result unable

to manage my own financial affairs, such written statement shall be attached to the original of this Power of Attorney.

4. I hereby grant (subject to the provisions of Clause 6) my Agent full power and authority over all my finances and property, both real and personal, and authorize my Agent to do and perform each and every act which I could do or perform and I hereby ratify and confirm all that my Agent shall do or cause to be done under this Power of Attorney.

5. Without prejudice to the provisions of Clause 4 but subject always to the provisions of Clause 6, my Agent's powers shall include, but shall not be limited to, the power to:

(a)   **Real property transactions**

receive from any person, to retain and to invest and reinvest in any kind of property or investment; to dispose of any property or any interest therein at such times and upon such terms and conditions as shall seem proper and to give good and sufficient instruments of transfer and to receive the proceeds of any such disposition; to purchase, manage, maintain and insure any property and to lease the same for such periods and on such terms as shall seem advantageous, and if advisable to pay for the value of any improvements made by a tenant under any such lease; to incur, extend or renew mortgage indebtedness; to make ordinary and extraordinary repairs and alterations to any building, to raze or erect buildings and to make improvements or to abandon any buildings or property; and to make any agreement of partition of such property and to give or receive money or other property in connection therewith;

(b)   **Personal property transactions**

buy, sell, mortgage, hypothecate, assign, transfer, grant options over and deal with all my personal property, tangible or intangible; and to manage, improve, repair and lease same; and to make, do, and transact all and every kind of business of whatever nature in respect thereto; and in each case in such manner and on such terms as my agent deems proper;

(c)   **Commercial transactions**

manage, sell, administer, liquidate, continue, discontinue or otherwise deal with any corporation, partnership or other business interest of mine as my Agent deems fit; to engage, compensate and discharge employees, agents, professional advisors and consultants; to assent to, oppose and participate in any reorganization, recapitalization, merger, consolidation or similar proceeding, to deposit securities, delegate discretionary powers, pay assessments or other expenses and exchange property, all as fully as might be done by persons owning similar property in their own right;

(d)   **Financial transactions**

open, administer, manage and close bank, savings, loans brokerage, and other such accounts in my name, to lodge proceeds to and withdraw proceeds from such accounts, to receive, draw, endorse and sign checks, bank drafts, bills of exchange, loan notes, promissory notes, letters of credit and certificates of deposit in relation to any such account and the proceeds therein; to pay any sums owing in respect of any such account, to use all credit cards issued in my name; to borrow such sums of money as my Agent may from time to time deem fit and to secure any such obligations by mortgage or pledge and to execute all documents in connection therewith;

(e)   **Financial securities**

purchase, exercise, surrender, transfer, sell or otherwise dispose of all rights, options, powers and privileges, and to vote in person or by proxy, in relation to any stocks, bonds or other securities, all as fully as might be done by persons owning similar property in their own right;

(f)   **Commodity and option transactions**

buy, sell, transfer and deal in commodities and options of all types; and to exercise all powers and do all matters and things incidental to the same;

(g)   **Insurance and annuity transactions**

exercise or perform any act or do anything in connection with any insurance cover I may have in my name (including, but not limited to, taking out new cover, paying premiums, making claims, extending cover, renewing polices and terminating policies) which my Agent deems necessary or prudent to maintain the value of my real or personal property;

(h)   **Estate and trust transactions**

demand, sue for, collect, and receive all legacies, bequests, and gifts due, payable or belonging to me, and take all lawful means, for the recovery thereof and to compromise the same and give discharges for the same; and to transfer any interest I may have in property, whether real or personal, tangible or intangible, to the trustee of any trust that I have created for my benefit;

(i)   **Retirement plans**

create and contribute to any type of retirement plan established in my name or for my benefit; to select any payment option under any retirement plan in which I am a participant or change options I have selected; to make voluntary contributions to such plans; to "roll-over" plan benefits into other retirement plans; to borrow money and purchase assets therefrom and sell assets thereto, if authorized by any such plan; to receive benefits from and engage in transactions (including the making of any plan election) with any retirement plan of which I am a beneficiary, and to exercise all powers necessary or desirable in connection with the maintenance and administration of such plans;

(j) **Family maintenance**

do all things and acts to maintain and support my family, including the making of any payments to and on behalf of my family that my Agent reasonably deems fit; and to hire accountants, attorneys at law, consultants, clerks, physicians, nurses, agents, servants, workmen, and others and to remove them, and to appoint others in their place, and to pay and allow the persons so employed such salaries, wages, or other remunerations, as my Agent shall deem proper;

(k) **Benefits**

prepare, execute and file any application or claim for any government, insurance, medical, military or social security benefit that I may be entitled to receive, to receive personal, confidential and medical information; to settle, compromise or contest any related assessments made against me; and to represent me in all matters relating to same;

(l) **Claims and litigation**

initiate, discontinue, defend and settle all actions, demands, claims and legal proceedings, by arbitration or otherwise, in connection with any or all of my real and personal property and any rights, interests or entitlements that I may have or any matters in which I am in any way concerned, in such manner as my Agent shall deem fit; and to give appropriate discharges, releases and receipt for the same;

(m) **Taxation**

prepare, execute and file any and all tax and informational returns that I may be entitled or required to make; to pay any taxes, surcharges and penalties duly owing by me, to file claims for tax refunds of every description; to settle, compromise or contest any tax assessments made against me; and to represent me in all matters before the Internal Revenue Service;

(n) **Safe deposit box**

access any safety deposit box registered in my name alone or jointly with others, and to remove any property or papers located therein; and

(o) **Deal with contracts**

enter into, negotiate, alter, amend, revoke, and exercise all rights granted under contracts of all types.

6. My Agent shall have no authority to give any of my property to, or to use any of my property for the benefit of, himself or herself. In addition, my agent (i) cannot execute a will, a codicil, or any will substitute on my behalf; (ii) cannot change the beneficiary on any life insurance policy that I own; (iii) cannot make gifts on my behalf; (iv) may not exercise any powers that would cause any assets of mine to be considered taxable to my agent or to my agent's estate for purposes of any income, estate, or inheritance tax, and (v) cannot contravene any medical or healthcare power of attorney or living will I have executed whether prior or subsequent to the execution of this Power of Attorney.

7. The powers conferred on my Agent herein may be exercised by my Agent alone, and my Agent's signature or act under the authority granted herein may be accepted by any third person or organization as fully authorized by me and with the same legal force and effect as if I were personally present, competent and acting on my own behalf.

8. Third parties may rely upon the representations of the Agent as to all matters regarding powers granted to the Agent. No person who acts in reliance on the authority granted under this Power of Attorney shall incur any liability to me or to my estate for permitting the Agent to exercise any power prior to actual knowledge that the Power of Attorney has been revoked or terminated by operation of law or otherwise.

9. No agent named or substituted in this Power of Attorney shall incur any liability to me for acting or refraining from acting under this power, except for such agent's own misconduct, fraud or negligence.

10. My Agent shall provide an accounting for all funds and assets handled and all acts performed as my Agent, if I so request or if such a request is made by any authorized personal representative or fiduciary properly acting on my behalf. My Agent shall not however be obliged to file any such accountings or any inventory with a court and any obligation in this respect is hereby waived to the fullest extent permitted by law.

11. My Agent shall be reimbursed for reasonable expenses incurred while acting as my Agent and may receive reasonable compensation for acting as Agent.

12. This power of attorney will be governed by the laws of the State of _____ without

regard for conflicts of laws principles and is intended to be valid in all jurisdictions of the United States of America and all foreign nations.

Executed this _____ day of _____, 20_____, at _____
_____.

_____
The Principal

Witness Affidavit

I declare, on the basis of information and belief, that the person who signed or acknowledged this document (the principal) is personally known to me, that he/she signed or acknowledged this Power of Attorney in my presence, and that he/she appears to be of sound mind and under no duress, fraud, or undue influence. I am not related to the principal by blood, marriage, or adoption, either as a spouse, a lineal ancestor, descendant of the parents of the principal, or spouse of any of them. I am not directly financially responsible for the principal's medical care. I am not entitled to any portion of the principal's estate upon his/her decease, whether under any Will or as an heir by intestate succession, nor am I the beneficiary of an insurance policy on the principal's life, nor do I have a claim against the principal's estate as of this time. I am not the principal's attending physician, nor an employee of the attending physician. No more than one witness is an employee of a health facility in which the principal is a patient. I am not appointed as Healthcare Agent or Successor Healthcare Agent by this document.

Witness No. 1
Signature: _____
Date: _____
Print Name: _____
Telephone: _____
Residence Address: _____
_____
_____
_____

Witness No. 2
Signature: _____
Date: _____
Print Name: _____

Telephone: _____

Residence Address: _____

_____

_____

_____

Notary Affidavit

State of _____   County of _____

On _____ before me, _____, a notary public, personally appeared _____, who proved to me on the basis of satisfactory evidence to be the person whose name is subscribed to the within instrument and acknowledged to me that he/she executed the same in his/her authorized capacity, and that by his/her signature on the instrument he/she executed the instrument. I certify under PENALTY OF PERJURY that the foregoing is true and correct. Witness my hand and official seal.

Signature: _____

Print Name: _____

My commission expires on: _____

(Seal)

Preparation Statement

This document was prepared by the following individual:

_____

Print Name

_____

Signature

Acknowledgment of Agent

By accepting or acting under the appointment, the agent assumes the fiduciary and other legal responsibilities of an agent.

_____

Print Name of Agent

_____

Signature of Agent

Limited Power of Attorney For Finance and Property

Downloadable Forms

Blank copies of all this form can be downloaded from the EstateBee website. Simply login to your account or, if you don't have an account, you can create one for free.

www.estate-bee.com/login

Once logged in, go to your profile page and enter the code listed below in the 'Use Codes' tab:

LPOAB1629

Dated this _____ day of _____, 20____

Limited Power of Attorney

of

_____

(Principal)

Notice: The powers granted by this document are broad and sweeping. If you have any questions about these powers, obtain competent legal advice. This document does not authorize anyone to make medical and other healthcare decisions for you. You may revoke this power of attorney if you later wish to do so provided you are of sound mind.

www.estate-bee.com

Limited Power of Attorney

1. I, _____ of _____ aged eighteen years and upwards hereby appoint _____ of _____ ___ as my lawfully appointed attorney in fact (referred to as the "Agent") on and subject to the terms and conditions set out below. If for any reason this person shall be unable or unwilling to act as my Agent, I hereby appoint _____ of _____ _____ to act as my Agent instead subject to the terms and conditions set out herein.

2. This power of attorney shall apply for financial and property applications only and shall remain effective until the earlier of (i) _____ days from the date hereof; (ii) the date of any written revocation of my Agent's authority hereunder; (iii) the date upon which my Agent has fulfilled the purpose set out in clause 5 hereof; (iv) the date on which I am determined to be incapacitated or (v) the date of my death.

3. This power of attorney shall become and is hereby effective immediately and will continue in full force and effect until terminated in accordance with the provisions of Clause 2. This power of attorney shall, for the avoidance of doubt, be construed as a limited power of attorney.

4. I hereby grant (subject to the provisions of Clause 5) my Agent full power and authority to do and perform each and every act which I could do or perform for the purpose(s) of _____

_____

_____

_____

_____

_____ and I hereby ratify and confirm all that my Agent shall do or cause to be done under this Power of Attorney.

5. My Agent shall have no authority to give any of my property to, or to use any of my property for the benefit of, himself or herself. In addition, my agent (i) cannot execute a will, a codicil, or any will substitute on my behalf; (ii) cannot change the beneficiary on any life insurance policy that I own; (iii) cannot make gifts on my behalf; (iv) may not exercise any powers that would cause any assets of mine to be considered taxable to my agent or to my agent's estate for purposes of any income, estate, or inheritance tax, and (v) cannot contravene any medical or healthcare power of attorney or living will I have executed whether prior or subsequent to the execution of this Power of Attorney.

6. The powers conferred on my Agent herein may be exercised by my Agent alone, and my Agent's signature or act under the authority granted herein may be accepted by any third person or organization as fully authorized by me and with the same legal force and effect as if I were personally present, competent and acting on my own behalf.

7. Third parties may rely upon the representations of the Agent as to all matters regarding

powers granted to the Agent. No person who acts in reliance on the authority granted under this Power of Attorney shall incur any liability to me or to my estate for permitting the Agent to exercise any power prior to actual knowledge that the Power of Attorney has been revoked or terminated by operation of law or otherwise.

8. No agent named or substituted in this Power of Attorney shall incur any liability to me for acting or refraining from acting under this power, except for such agent's own misconduct, fraud, or negligence.

9. My Agent shall provide an accounting for all funds and assets handled and all acts performed as my Agent, if I so request or if such a request is made by any authorized personal representative or fiduciary properly acting on my behalf. My Agent shall not however be obliged to file any such accountings or any inventory with a court and any obligation in this respect is hereby waived to the fullest extent permitted by law.

10. My Agent shall be reimbursed for reasonable expenses incurred while acting as my Agent and may receive reasonable compensation for acting as Agent.

11. This power of attorney will be governed by the laws of the State of _____ without regard for conflicts of laws principles and is intended to be valid in all jurisdictions of the United States of America and all foreign nations.

Executed this _____ day of _____, 20_____, at _____
_____
_____.

_____
The Principal

Witness Affidavit

I declare, on the basis of information and belief, that the person who signed or acknowledged this document (the principal) is personally known to me, that he/she signed or acknowledged this Power of Attorney in my presence, and that he/she appears to be of sound mind and under no duress, fraud, or undue influence. I am not related to the principal by blood, marriage, or adoption, either as a spouse, a lineal ancestor, descendant of the parents of the principal, or spouse of any of them. I am not directly financially responsible for the principal's medical care. I am not entitled to any portion of the principal's estate upon his/her decease, whether under any Will or as an heir by intestate succession, nor am I the beneficiary of an insurance policy on the principal's life, nor do I have a claim against the principal's estate as of this time. I am not the principal's attending physician, nor an employee of the attending physician. No more than one witness is an employee of a health facility in which the principal is a patient. I am not appointed as Healthcare Agent or Successor Healthcare Agent by this document.

Witness No. 1

Signature: _____

Date: _____

Print Name: _____

Telephone: _____

Residence Address: _____

_____

_____

_____

Witness No. 2

Signature: _____

Date: _____

Print Name: _____

Telephone: _____

Residence Address: _____

_____

_____

_____

Notary Affidavit

State of _____   County of _____

On _____ before me, _____, a notary public, personally appeared _____, who proved to me on the basis of satisfactory evidence to be the person whose name is subscribed to the within instrument and acknowledged to me that he/she executed the same in his/her authorized capacity, and that by his/her signature on the instrument he/she executed the instrument. I certify under PENALTY OF PERJURY that the foregoing is true and correct. Witness my hand and official seal.

Signature: _____

Print Name: _____

My commission expires on: _____

(Seal)

Preparation Statement

This document was prepared by the following individual:

_____

Print Name

_____

Signature

Acknowledgment of Agent

By accepting or acting under the appointment, the agent assumes the fiduciary and other legal responsibilities of an agent.

_____

Print Name of Agent

_____

Signature of Agent

Durable Limited Power of Attorney For Finance and Property

Downloadable Forms

Blank copies of all this form can be downloaded from the EstateBee website. Simply login to your account or, if you don't have an account, you can create one for free.

www.estate-bee.com/login

Once logged in, go to your profile page and enter the code listed below in the 'Use Codes' tab:

DLPOAB1629

Dated this _____ day of _____, 20____

_____

Durable Limited Power of Attorney

of

_____

(Principal)

Notice: The powers granted by this document are broad and sweeping. If you have any questions about these powers, obtain competent legal advice. This document does not authorize anyone to make medical and other healthcare decisions for you. You may revoke this power of attorney if you later wish to do so provided you are of sound mind.

www.estate-bee.com

Durable Limited Power of Attorney

1. I, _____ of _____ aged
eighteen years and upwards hereby appoint _____ of _____
_____ as my lawfully appointed attorney in fact (referred to as the "Agent") on and
subject to the terms and conditions set out below. If for any reason this person shall be unable
or unwilling to act as my Agent, I hereby appoint _____ of _____
_____ to act as my Agent instead subject to the terms and conditions set out herein.

2. This durable limited power of attorney shall apply for financial and property applications
only, shall not be affected by my subsequent disability or incapacity and shall remain
effective until the earlier of (i) _____ days from the date hereof; (ii) the date of any written
revocation of my Agent's authority hereunder; (iii) the date upon which my Agent has
fulfilled the purpose set out in clause 5 hereof; or (iv) the date of my death.

3. I direct that this durable limited power of attorney shall become effective in the manner that I
have expressed below:-

(initial only one option below)

_____ This durable power of attorney is hereby effective immediately and shall continue
in full force and effect until it is terminated in accordance with clause 2 hereof. This
power of attorney shall be construed as a durable limited power of attorney and shall
continue to be effective even if I become disabled, incapacitated, or incompetent.

_____ This durable power of attorney shall, subject to clause 2, become effective only in the
event that I become mentally incapacitated or disabled so that as a result I am not able
to manage my financial affairs in which case it shall become effective as of the date
of the written statement to be provided by a physician pursuant to the terms of this
Clause 3. If this power of attorney becomes effective, it shall remain effective during
any period in which I am incapacitated or disabled until terminated in accordance
with clause 2.

The determination of whether I have become incapacitated or disabled so that I am not
able to manage my financial affairs shall be made in writing by a licensed physician; if
practical, this physician shall be _____ of _____

_____ or failing him/her any licensed physician having been at least ten years in practice.

In the event that a licensed physician has made a written determination pursuant to this Clause 3 that I have become incapacitated or disabled and as a result unable to manage my own financial affairs, such written statement shall be attached to the original of this Power of Attorney.

4. I hereby grant (subject to the provisions of Clause 5) my Agent full power and authority to do and perform each and every act which I could do or perform for the purpose(s) of _____

_____

_____

_____

_____ and I hereby ratify and confirm all that my Agent shall do or cause to be done under this Power of Attorney.

5. My Agent shall have no authority to give any of my property to, or to use any of my property for the benefit of, himself or herself. In addition, my agent (i) cannot execute a will, a codicil, or any will substitute on my behalf; (ii) cannot change the beneficiary on any life insurance policy that I own; (iii) cannot make gifts on my behalf; (iv) may not exercise any powers that would cause any assets of mine to be considered taxable to my agent or to my agent's estate for purposes of any income, estate, or inheritance tax, and (v) cannot contravene any medical or healthcare power of attorney or living will I have executed whether prior or subsequent to the execution of this Power of Attorney.

6. The powers conferred on my Agent herein may be exercised by my Agent alone, and my Agent's signature or act under the authority granted herein may be accepted by any third person or organization as fully authorized by me and with the same legal force and effect as if I were personally present, competent and acting on my own behalf.

7. Third parties may rely upon the representations of the Agent as to all matters regarding powers granted to the Agent. No person who acts in reliance on the authority granted under this Power of Attorney shall incur any liability to me or to my estate for permitting the Agent to exercise any power prior to actual knowledge that the Power of Attorney has been revoked or terminated by operation of law or otherwise.

8. No agent named or substituted in this Power of Attorney shall incur any liability to me for acting or refraining from acting under this power, except for such agent's own misconduct, fraud or negligence.

9. My Agent shall provide an accounting for all funds and assets handled and all acts performed as my Agent, if I so request or if such a request is made by any authorized personal representative or fiduciary properly acting on my behalf. My Agent shall not however be obliged to file any such accountings or any inventory with a court and any obligation in this respect is hereby waived to the fullest extent permitted by law.

10. My Agent shall be reimbursed for reasonable expenses incurred while acting as my Agent and may receive reasonable compensation for acting as Agent.

11. This power of attorney will be governed by the laws of the State of _____ without regard for conflicts of laws principles and is intended to be valid in all jurisdictions of the United States of America and all foreign nations.

Executed this _____ day of _____, 20_____, at _____
_____.

_____
The Principal

Witness Affidavit

I declare, on the basis of information and belief, that the person who signed or acknowledged this document (the principal) is personally known to me, that he/she signed or acknowledged this Power of Attorney in my presence, and that he/she appears to be of sound mind and under no duress, fraud, or undue influence. I am not related to the principal by blood, marriage, or adoption, either as a spouse, a lineal ancestor, descendant of the parents of the principal, or spouse of any of them. I am not directly financially responsible for the principal's medical care. I am not entitled to any portion of the principal's estate upon his/her decease, whether under any Will or as an heir by intestate succession, nor am I the beneficiary of an insurance policy on the principal's life, nor do I have a claim against the principal's estate as of this time. I am not the principal's attending physician, nor an employee of the attending physician. No more than one witness is an employee of a health facility in which the principal is a patient. I am not appointed as Healthcare Agent or Successor Healthcare Agent by this document.

Witness No. 1

Signature: _____

Date: _____

Print Name: _____

Telephone: _____

Residence Address: _____

_____

_____

_____

Witness No. 2

Signature: _____

Date: _____

Print Name: _____

Telephone: _____

Residence Address: _____

_____

_____

_____

Notary Affidavit

State of _____ **County of** _____

On _____ before me, _____, a notary public, personally appeared _____, who proved to me on the basis of satisfactory evidence to be the person whose name is subscribed to the within instrument and acknowledged to me that he/she executed the same in his/her authorized capacity, and that by his/her signature on the instrument he/she executed the instrument. I certify under PENALTY OF PERJURY that the foregoing is true and correct. Witness my hand and official seal.

Signature: _____

Print Name: _____

My commission expires on: _____

(Seal)

Preparation Statement

This document was prepared by the following individual:

_____

Print Name

_____

Signature

Acknowledgment of Agent

By accepting or acting under the appointment, the agent assumes the fiduciary and other legal responsibilities of an agent.

_____

Print Name of Agent

_____

Signature of Agent

Appendix 4

Agent's Acceptance of Appointment

Agent's Acceptance of Appointment
(For Use in Georgia Only)

Downloadable Forms

Blank copies of all this form can be downloaded from the EstateBee website. Simply login to your account or, if you don't have an account, you can create one for free.

www.estate-bee.com/login

Once logged in, go to your profile page and enter the code listed below in the 'Use Codes' tab:

AAAPOAB1629

Acceptance of Appointment

I, _____ (print name), have read the foregoing Power of Attorney and am the person identified therein as Agent for _____ (name of grantor of power of attorney), the Principal named therein. I hereby acknowledge the following:

(i)   I owe a duty of loyalty and good faith to the Principal and must use the powers granted to me only for the benefit of the Principal.

(ii) I must keep the Principal's funds and other assets separate and apart from my funds and other assets and titled in the name of the Principal. I must not transfer title to any of the Principal's funds or other assets into my name alone. My name must not be added to the title of any funds or other assets of the Principal, unless I am specifically designated as Agent for the Principal in the title.

(iii) I must protect, conserve, and exercise prudence and caution in my dealings with the Principal's funds and other assets.

(iv) I must keep a full and accurate record of my acts, receipts, and disbursements on behalf of the Principal, and be ready to account to the Principal for such acts, receipts, and disbursements at all times. I must provide an annual accounting to the Principal of my acts, receipts, and disbursements, and must furnish an accounting of such acts, receipts, and disbursements to the personal representative of the Principal's estate within 90 days after the date of death of the Principal.

I have read the Compensation of Agent paragraph in the Power of Attorney and agree to abide by it.

I acknowledge my authority to act on behalf of the Principal ceases at the death of the Principal.

I hereby accept the foregoing appointment as Agent for the Principal with full knowledge of the responsibilities imposed on me, and I will faithfully carry out my duties to the best of my ability.

Dated:_____, _____.

(Signature)_____
(Address)_____

Note: A notarized signature is not required unless the Principal has included instructions regarding property transactions.

I, _____, a Notary Public, do hereby certify that _____ _____ personally appeared before me this date and acknowledged the due execution of the foregoing Acceptance of Appointment.

_____

Notary Public

Appendix 5

Durable Power of Attorney for Healthcare & Living Will

Durable Power of Attorney for Healthcare & Living Will

Downloadable Forms

Blank copies of this Durable Power of Attorney for Healthcare & Living Will form can be downloaded from the EstateBee website. Simply login to your account or, if you don't have an account, you can create one for free.

www.estate-bee.com/login

Once logged in, go to your profile page and enter the code listed below in the 'Use Codes' tab:

DHPOAB1629

Durable Power of Attorney for Healthcare & Living Will

of

_____

(The Principal)

Dated this _____ day of _____, 20____

www.estate-bee.com

Durable Power of Attorney for Healthcare & Living Will

I, _____ of _____ , being of sound and disposing mind and having attained the age of majority in the state of _____ _____ make this Durable Power of Attorney for Healthcare & Living Will.

Part 1 - Durable Power of Attorney for Healthcare Decisions

1. **Designation of Agent**

1.1 I appoint the following individual as my primary agent:

Name: _____

Address: _____

        _____

        _____

        _____

Home Telephone: _____

Work Telephone: _____

1.2 If I revoke my primary agent's authority or if my primary agent is not willing, able, or reasonably available to make a healthcare decision for me, then I appoint the following individual as my alternate agent to make such decisions on behalf:

Name: _____

Address: _____

        _____

        _____

        _____

Home Telephone: _____

Work Telephone: _____

1.3 If I revoke the authority of my primary agent and my first named alternate agent or if neither is willing, able, or reasonably available to make a healthcare decision for me, then I appoint the following individual as my alternate agent to make such decisions on my behalf:

Name: _____

Address: _____

_____

_____

_____

Home Telephone: _____

Work Telephone: _____

2. Agent's Authority

2.1 I hereby authorize and direct my agent to follow my individual instructions and my other wishes to the extent known to the agent in making all healthcare decisions for me. If these are not known to my agent, then my agent is authorized to make these decisions in accordance with my best interests, including decisions to provide, withhold, or withdraw artificial hydration and nutrition and other forms of healthcare to keep me alive, except as I otherwise state herein:

Note: *In each of (i) to (iv) below, initial one choice only in each section.*

(i)   _____   I grant my agent power to withhold or withdraw life-prolonging procedures in accordance with my instructions herein.

_____ I do not grant my agent power to withhold or withdraw life-prolonging procedures.

(ii)   _____ I grant my agent power to withhold or withdraw artificial hydration and nutrition in accordance with my instructions herein.

_____ I do not grant my agent power to withhold or withdraw artificial hydration and nutrition.

(iii)   _____ I grant my agent the power of control over the disposal of my remains and organ donation decisions subject to my instructions herein.

_____ I do not grant my agent any power of control over the disposal of my remains and organ donation decisions.

(iv)   _____ I grant my agent the power to consent to or refuse an autopsy being carried out on my remains.

_____ I do not grant my agent the power to consent to or to refuse an autopsy being carried out on my remains.

(v)   _____

_____

_____

_____

_____

_____

_____

_____

_____

3. When Agent's Authority Becomes Effective

3.1 My agent's authority shall become effective when my primary physician, or in the case of emergency an attending physician, determines that I am unable to make my own healthcare decisions.

4. Agent's Obligation

4.1 My agent shall make healthcare decisions for me in accordance with the instructions set out herein and my other wishes to the extent known to my agent. To the extent my wishes are unknown; my agent shall make healthcare decisions for me in accordance with what my agent determines to be in my best interest. In determining my best interest, my agent shall consider my personal values to the extent known to my agent.

4.2 Accordingly, save as may be provided herein, my agent is authorized as follows:

(a) to consent, refuse, or withdraw consent to any and all types of medical care, treatment, surgical procedures, diagnostic procedures, medication, and the use of mechanical or other procedures that affect any bodily function, including, but not limited to, artificial respiration, nutritional support and hydration, and cardiopulmonary resuscitation;

(b) to authorize, or refuse to authorize, any medication or procedure intended to relieve pain, even though such use may lead to physical damage, addiction, or hasten the moment of, but not intentionally cause, my death;

(c) to authorize my admission to or discharge, even against medical advice, from any hospital, nursing care facility, or similar facility or service;

(d) to take any other action necessary to making, documenting, and assuring implementation of decisions concerning my healthcare, including, but not limited to, granting any waiver or release from liability required by any hospital, physician, nursing care provider, or other healthcare provider; signing any documents relating to refusals of treatment or the leaving of a facility against medical advice, and pursuing any legal action in my name, and at the expense of my estate to force compliance with my wishes as determined by my agent, or to seek actual or punitive damages for the failure to comply; and

(e) to request, review, and receive any information, verbal or written, regarding my physical or mental health, including, but not limited to, medical and hospital records and to consent to the disclosure of this information.

5. **Nomination of Guardian**

5.1 If a court determines that a guardian of my person should be appointed for me, then I nominate my primary agent as my guardian. If my primary agent is unable or unwilling to act as my guardian, then I nominate the alternate agent(s) whom I have named under clause 1 above, in the order designated, as my guardian. No guardian appointed hereunder shall be required to post bond.

Part 2 - Instructions for Healthcare

6. **End-of-Life Decisions**

6.1 Except to the extent prohibited by law, I direct that my healthcare providers and others involved in my care provide, withhold, or withdraw treatment in accordance with the choices I have expressed below:

(initial only those options which apply)

<u>Terminal Condition</u>

____ If, at any time, I have a medical condition certified to be a terminal condition by two physicians who have personally examined me, and the physicians have determined that my death could occur within a reasonably short period of time without the use of life-sustaining procedures then I direct that, save as may be set out herein, such life-sustaining procedures

(initial only the option immediately below which you want to apply)

_____SHALL   _____ SHALL NOT

be applied to prolong my life within the limits of generally accepted healthcare standards.

Specifically, and notwithstanding the foregoing, if I am suffering from a terminal condition I want to receive those treatments which I have initialed below and do not want to receive those which I have not initialed below:

(initial only the treatments below you want to receive)

_____ artificial nutrition or hydration.

_____cardiac resuscitation or a cardiac pacemaker.

_____blood or blood products.

_____mechanical respiration.

_____kidney dialysis.

_____antibiotics.

_____any form of surgery or invasive diagnostic tests.

_____organs.

Permanent Unconsciousness

____   If, at any time, I have a medical condition certified to be a terminal condition by two physicians who have personally examined me, and the physicians have certified that I am in a state of permanent unconsciousness and the application of life-sustaining procedures would serve only to prolong the dying process then I direct that, save as may be set out herein, such life-sustaining procedures

(initial only the option immediately below which you want to apply)

_____SHALL   _____ SHALL NOT

be applied to prolong my life within the limits of generally accepted healthcare standards.

Specifically, and notwithstanding the foregoing, if I am in a persistent vegetative state or other condition of permanent unconsciousness I want to receive those treatments which I have initialed below and do not want to receive those which I have not initialed below:

(initial only the treatments below you want to receive)

_____ artificial nutrition or hydration.

_____ cardiac resuscitation or a cardiac pacemaker.

_____blood or blood products.

_____mechanical respiration.

_____kidney dialysis.

_____antibiotics.

_____any form of surgery or invasive diagnostic tests.

_____organs.

Maximum Treatment

____   I want to receive the maximum treatment in all possible circumstances to prolong my life.

7. **Relief from Pain**

    (initial one choice only)

    _____I want to receive treatment for the alleviation of pain or discomfort.

    _____I do not want to receive treatment for the alleviation of pain or discomfort.

8. **Pregnancy (Optional)**

    (If applicable, initial your choice below. If no choice is initialed, this clause shall cease to apply)

8.1 Should I become unconscious and I am pregnant, I direct that the end-of-life provisions in this document shall, unless applicable laws prescribe otherwise:

    (initial one choice below)

    _____continue to have full effect.

    _____cease to have full effect.

Part 3 - Anatomical Gifts

9. **Anatomical Gift at Death (Optional)**

    (If applicable, initial your choice below. If no choice is initialed, this clause shall cease to apply)

9.1 Upon my death:

    _____ I do not wish to give any organs, tissues or other body parts and refuse to make an anatomical gift.

    or

    _____ I hereby give any needed organs, tissues, or other body parts.

    or

    _____ I give the following organs, tissues, or other body parts only:-

    _____
    _____
    _____
    _____
    _____.

9.2 If I have decided to donate organs in 9.1 above, then my gift shall be for the initialed purposes below only:

    _____Transplant.

    _____Therapy.

____ Research.

____ Education.

Part 4 - Primary Physician

10. Primary Physician

10.1 I appoint _____ of _____ (Telephone:- _____) as my primary physician. If the aforementioned physician is unable or unwilling to act as my primary physician, then I appoint _____ of _____ (Telephone:- _____) as my alternate physician. If neither of the foregoing are willing and able to act as my primary physician, my primary physician shall be deemed to be the lead physician advising on my medical treatment.

Part 5 - General

11. Effect of Copy

11.1 A copy of this form has the same effect as the original.

I sign my name to this Durable Power of Attorney for Healthcare & Living Will on this _____ day of _____, 20_____ at _____ in the State of _____ _____.

_____

Signature of Principal

Witness Affidavit

I declare, on the basis of information and belief, that the person who signed or acknowledged this document (the principal) is personally known to me (or has proven their identity to me), that he/she signed or acknowledged this Durable Power of Attorney for Healthcare & Living Will in my presence, and that he/she appears to be of sound mind and under no duress, fraud, or undue influence. I am not related to the principal by blood, marriage, or adoption, either as a spouse, a lineal ancestor, descendant of the parents of the principal, or spouse of any of them. I am not directly financially responsible for the principal's medical care. I am not entitled to any portion of the principal's estate upon his/her decease, whether under any will or as an heir by intestate succession, nor am I the beneficiary of an insurance policy on the principal's life, nor do I have a claim against the principal's estate as of this time. I am not the principal's attending physician, nor an employee of the attending physician. No more than one witness is an employee of a health facility in which the principal is a patient. I am not appointed as a healthcare agent or successor healthcare agent by this document.

Witness No. 1

Signature: _____

Date: _____

Print Name: _____

Telephone: _____

Residence Address: _____

_____

_____

_____

Witness No. 2

Signature: _____

Date: _____

Print Name: _____

Telephone: _____

Residence Address: _____

_____

_____

_____

Notary Affidavit

State of _____   County of _____

On _____ before me, _____, a notary public, personally appeared _____, who proved to me on the basis of satisfactory evidence to be the person whose name is subscribed to the within instrument and acknowledged to me that he/she executed the same in his/her authorized capacity, and that by his/her signature on the instrument he/she executed the instrument. I certify under PENALTY OF PERJURY that the foregoing is true and correct. Witness my hand and official seal.

Signature: _____

Print Name: _____

My commission expires on: _____

(Seal)

Appendix 6

Notice of Revocation of Power of Attorney

Notice of Revocation of a Power of Attorney

Downloadable Forms

Blank copies of all this form can be downloaded from the EstateBee website. Simply login to your account or, if you don't have an account, you can create one for free.

www.estate-bee.com/login

Once logged in, go to your profile page and enter the code listed below in the 'Use Codes' tab:

REVPOAB1629

Dated this _____ day of _____, 20___

_____

Notice of Revocation

of

_____
(Principal)

_____

EstateBee

www.estate-bee.com

Notice of Revocation

I, _____ of _____ aged
eighteen years and upwards hereby revoke, countermand and make null and void the Power of
Attorney dated _____ (the "Power of Attorney") and granted in favor of __
_____ (the "Agent", which expression shall include any successor
agent appointed under the Power of Attorney) and all rights, powers and authority thereby given
to the Agent shall hereby lapse and cease.

Executed this _____ day of _____, 20 _____, at _____
_____.

_____
The Principal

Witness Affidavit

I declare, on the basis of information and belief, that the person who signed or acknowledged
this document (the principal) is personally known to me, that he/she signed or acknowledged
this Notice of Revocation of a Power of Attorney in my presence, and that he/she appears to be
of sound mind and under no duress, fraud, or undue influence. I am not related to the principal
by blood, marriage, or adoption, either as a spouse, a lineal ancestor, descendant of the parents of
the principal, or spouse of any of them. I am not directly financially responsible for the principal's
medical care. I am not entitled to any portion of the principal's estate upon his/her decease,
whether under any Will or as an heir by intestate succession, nor am I the beneficiary of an
insurance policy on the principal's life, nor do I have a claim against the principal's estate as of this
time. I am not the principal's attending physician, nor an employee of the attending physician. No
more than one witness is an employee of a health facility in which the principal is a patient. I am
not appointed as Healthcare Agent or Successor Healthcare Agent by this document.

Witness No. 1

Signature: _____

Date: _____

Print Name: _____

Telephone: _____

Residence Address: _____

_____

_____

_____

Witness No. 2

Signature: _____

Date: _____

Print Name: _____

Telephone: _____

Residence Address: _____

_____

_____

_____

Notary Affidavit

State of _____   County of _____

On _____ before me, _____, a notary public, personally appeared _____, who proved to me on the basis of satisfactory evidence to be the person whose name is subscribed to the within instrument and acknowledged to me that he/she executed the same in his/her authorized capacity, and that by his/her signature on the instrument he/she executed the instrument. I certify under PENALTY OF PERJURY that the foregoing is true and correct. Witness my hand and official seal.

Signature: _____

Print Name: _____

My commission expires on: _____

(Seal)

EstateBee's Estate Planning Range

Make Your Own
Last Will & Testament

Make Your Own
Living Trust & Avoid
Probate

Make Your Own
Medical & Financial
Power of Attorney

How to Probate an
Estate - A Step-by-Step
Guide for Executors

Estate Planning
Essentials - A Step-by-
Step Guide to Estate
Planning

Funeral Planning Basics
– A Step-by-Step Guide
to Funeral Planning

Legal Will Kit

Living Trust Kit

Healthcare Power of
Attorney & Living
Will Kit

Codicil to a Last
Will & Testament Kit

Durable General
Power of Attorney Kit

Durable Limited
Power of Attorney Kit

Made in United States
Orlando, FL
20 August 2022

21300801R00091